Clearly Ambiguous

John R. Nelson

ISBN: 1463535562
ISBN-13: 978-1463535568

DEDICATION

To my wife for encouraging me to pursue my writing. To Bob Lott, my friend for providing an outlet and the opportunity to pontificate my opinions via *The Observer* each week.

*

CONTENTS

ACKNOWLEDGEMENTS

Every week my wife, LeeAnn, patiently listens, comments, critiques, and inspires me to improve when I read my column to her. The publisher and editors at *The Observer* gave me the opportunity to write and share my thoughts every week. I appreciate all of the feedback from the Lott's, and Robert Burns. With confidence I was able to take what I had done at *The Observer* and start submitting to the *White County News*, thank you Billy Chism for taking a chance on me. Last but not least are the readers who pass comments to the editors and occasionally to me, thank you.

The adage, "In the land of the blind, the one-eyed man is king," is generally attributed to Desiderius Erasmus (1466-1536).

1 INTRODUCTION

I hated my English class in high school. Ironically as I have aged I found myself having to write for work whether generating proposals, contracts, or general correspondence. It is from this dislike that my desire to start writing for pleasure grew.

Several years ago I started my first book and have always joked, "I am eight pages into seven different books." I never seemed able to keep my thoughts coherent and translate my great ideas to paper. Driving down the road I constantly daydream and build incredible fictional plots in my head. However, as soon as I lay pencil to paper the visions evaporate and I find myself staring at a blank white computer screen or a tablet with nothing. I have tried dictation, an interesting method, but again my thoughts and what I read back never match.

My first writing effort was fondly referred to as my "manifesto." I dismissed this with laughter until I re-read the document several times. Ironically as I look back now, and you do too in this book, the prophetic nature of the thoughts is eerie. But, the content and methodology were far too scattered to make a good writer out of me.

Finally, I was leaving a funeral of a friend and felt compelled to capture my thoughts about "Death and Taxes." It was this first attempt and spewing forth my opinions that provided me the opportunity to write a weekly newspaper column. My friend Bob Lott would meet a group of friends at the "OM Bar" in New Smyrna Beach, Florida on Thursday afternoons to solve the world's problems. I was invited often to "men's club" to discuss issues but found myself busy or wanting to head home to family. After capturing my ideas on paper for "Death and Taxes" I shared a copy with Bob, the first time I felt confident to show someone else my writing. Immediately he offered to share it with the group, anonymously under the guise of an internet forward or download.

I remember that evening watching the copy passed around; my writing inspiring conversation and for the first time I was not criticized as a writer, like 10th grade English class, but debated and critiqued. When the group learned who wrote the short opinion I was praised and encouraged to continue.

Around the same time there were changes with our local newspaper, *The Observer* in New Smyrna Beach and Bob was part of the ownership group. Thus, I was afforded the opportunity to write weekly for the paper and from there began this book.

One question I am often asked is, "what kind of column do you write?"

My reply is short, and descriptive, "I cover politics, civil rights and freedoms, and essentially pontificate my position regarding what is wrong in America."

I was originally billed in *The Observer* as "The Man in the Middle." However, that is probably far from the truth as I personally have looked over two plus years of columns and see an obvious position; I am confident you will too.

2 MY VIEW OF THE WORLD

Duck! It's a Flying Car! (9/2/2009)

I was born in 1967, at the height of the hippie counter culture during the summer of love. The war in Vietnam was escalating, but was not quite an evening presence in our living rooms. As a nation we were focused on getting to the moon and beating back the Soviets. A computer filled a room, but had less computing power than today's digital watches. A color TV was an expensive marvel and "Made in Japan" was synonymous with "cheap".

As a child in the early 1970's, Evil Knevil was idolized, I saw television shows such as Star Trek and repeats of "Lost in Space". I remember seeing the Bell Telephone book with pictures of people talking in the future on videophones and could not wait to go to Disney World to fill my head with more images of "Tomorrow land". The year 2000 was so far away, but yet full of promises that we would be driving flying cars, watching TV on walls, and living on the moon. Doors would open and close with sounds as we approached them, lights would activate automatically, and we would talk to computers; living like George Jetson.

Some parts of that vision have come true as I do have flat panel televisions that hang like pictures, carry a communicator (cell-phone) in my pocket, not unlike "James T. Kirk", and motion detectors open store doors and turn lights on and off. But the other technologic visions have escaped us. I traded my SUV two years ago, a vehicle which weighed as much as my Dad's 1969 Ford Galaxy, and averaged the same gas mileage. In 35years we have accomplished little more in our ability to achieve a presence on the moon than where we were in 1973; having had no man step foot on our orbiting satellite since the last, Gene Cernan, left his mark.

On one hand, we have done so many things well: advances in medicine such as artificial hearts, efficiencies in agricultural, computers for the masses, and less costly access to education and travel. At the same time, our near God-like abilities have blinded us to changes taking place around us and created a near mass delusional acceptance of our abilities. The average American is more concerned with Britney Spears than the presidential election, last night's sports scores more than yesterday's stock market, and planning a summer vacation than events in hostile world regions.

Natural disasters have struck several times in this country in the last decade demonstrating the average citizen cannot care for himself. Hurricane Katrina and its images of personal lollygagging without the wherewithal to save one's self is an excellent example. I would assert the average person believes food comes from a can and has no understanding of how to care for himself. Other disasters such as flood, mass power failures, and California earthquakes have further driven home this problem that we are no longer the conquerors of technology and environment but have been conquered by our own success.

I want my flying car. I want the promises that were made to me as a kid by the generation that I am now paying social security to out of my paycheck. I want those advances to move forward and allow us to live on the moon and leave this planet. Instead, checks are being written that will further indebt out nation to others and ultimately force is back to a pre-industrialized agrarian society. Via increased energy costs, government bailouts, and trade deficits we are transferring our wealth to other nations and ultimately onto the backs of our children. In my opinion, it is more likely that we will be riding horses than driving flying cars in the future.

Taking a Break (10/28/2009)

One thing about living in Florida is how easy it is to fall victim to the sensationalism of hurricane reporting by local television stations. We crave wanting to know where Anna, Bill, Claudette and any of our other alphabetical list of storms is headed. It is nearly impossible to escape this invasion of news as the ticker or radar picture instantly showing location, intensity, and projected path of destruction is always on once the storm has been announced. This information invades our lives through print, computers, radio, television, and even local conversation.

I would argue that our lives in general have become much the same way regarding all news. In ancient times (before the 1980s), there were three networks, a public TV station, and changing channels necessitated getting off the couch so our exposure to the news was much more limited. Sure, an AM radio station typically played hourly updates, but our news was only available in the morning, at noon, or on the major networks in the evening. Paul Harvey was the extent of opinion and we recognized him as an entertainer. At night, Johnny Carson poked fun at events of the day, but the monologue was respectful and limited. Now, even local television stations now run two hours of "news" in the evening. Ironically, most of the news is not news though, but polling data reports, conjecture, and opinions.

You're reading this paper, this page of the paper, and this article. Most likely, like me you enjoy the news and keeping up with information. Recently I realized though, like hurricane news, the political and economic information I enjoy is changing at a slower pace than I desire. I found myself wanting more, craving more and starving for the latest news tidbit to radically change the political landscape. Each day I regularly visit web sites to read newspapers and review news sources. Fortunately, I cancelled cable television over a year ago and am no longer bombarded by the pontificates on different networks sharing their opinions, not reporting news.

Recently, I realized I was feeling a level of anxiety. Nothing bad, nothing in particular caused me anxiety. But instead, like the ongoing threat of a hurricane offshore that will more than likely miss central Florida, I felt the same anxiety watching the news and waiting, anticipating, and starving for the next story detailing some miniscule change in the health care debate or the current economic environment. Thus, I decided to take a break.

This past Sunday I told my wife that my goal for the week was to avoid the "news". No web sites, no talk radio, no seeking of information that I had no control over and could not impact. However, out of fairness, if I encountered news I would absorb it. So far my experience has been refreshing, like a vacation. I realized I could break my addiction and habit to seeking and looking for news. The next time a hurricane is coming I suggest you try it. A once a day check of conditions is more than adequate. The same holds true for most your exposure to talk radio, cable news, or evening network news. Once a day, read the paper or watch the news. Minute by minute; remember you are subjecting yourself to opinion and conjecture. It's not worth your time.

Me, Presidential Advisor (12/2/2009)

I have friends and family with whom I share thoughts, articles, and email forwards. I love being challenged on my positions and, more so, love the opportunity to truly express my opinions. Recently, my sister challenged me regarding one of our email exchanges. In particular, she asked "What would you do today if you were President or you could advise the President and he would do what you advised?"

Personally, I did not find this a difficult question at all, but I still gave it thought as I typed an email back to her. I never expected to include it in a column, but as she read through it and, surprisingly, supported most of my response I was excited to offer my advice to the President or anyone that will listen. I always approach every problem with the idea that debate will surround the issues because I believe this process finds the best solution. No party should be locked out from debate nor should any party exercise a majority position to unilaterally impose a platform. I believe these are the most important issues that need attention and would work to affect legislation to bring about changes:

First, I would require the constitution to be studied and enforced. Every nominee for political office in the land, regardless of position, would be given a copy of the Constitution and tested to qualify to hold office.

Second, I would move for term limits for all elected positions. I find it ironic that the President is the only federally elected position with term limits, whereas the House and Senate may hold positions for life. It is the abuse of power, and funding that occurs when instead a Congressman earns six times what the average American earns for working one-half as much and should be humbled to serve the American people. I believe no one should serve a lifetime like Byrd, Kennedy, Hollings, or Thurmond.

Third, like treason, I would move to make ethics violations, misappropriations, or unlawfulness by government officials (elected, appointed, and employed) subject to the death penalty. I believe only such consequence will return the qualities we seek in those who work for us.

Fourth, I would move to repeal laws from A to Z. Stimulus and health bills of 1,200 and 1,900 pages, respectively, are filled with legalese to protect special interests. No law should require more than ten pages. This would reduce wasteful programs and bureaucracy, saving the country huge sums of money.

Fifth, I would simplify the tax code to, at most, 5-10 pages long. I support all citizens, regardless of income, pay a tax (income, VAT, etc) for defense, roads, infrastructure. But, the tax system should not be used for social engineering, special programs, and promoting the rights of one citizen, rich or poor, above those of another.

Lastly, I would do everything possible to re-establish the sovereignty of the United States. I am not apologetic to other countries in the world for the actions our country has taken to set a model of freedom and democracy craved by citizens of the world. What we once had as liberty gave the rest of the world reason to believe in pursuing their own freedoms and America made herself available to support democracies.

Happy New Year (1/6/2010)

Many of us are taking a look at the last year and reflecting on what we did right and wrong and how to improve for 2010. I hope our government is doing the same, taking this time to reflect and improve its performance. Annually I make goals, not resolutions, but goals. After making a list of goals I prioritize and determine the actionable items needed to succeed. Unfortunately, I feel our government and country fall short similarly because there is no long-term vision, no goal. In contrast, President Kennedy did an excellent job of creating direction for the country when he set a goal of putting a man on the moon before 1970. Since then our Presidents have spoken in grandiose prose with no answerability thus allowing them to avoid political failure.

The past year, with a new administration, and significantly reshaped Congress offers an excellent opportunity for reflection. One year ago today we had no stimulus plan, no healthcare plan, no Copenhagen Agreement, and less troops committed to Afghanistan. At the same time, the U-6 unemployment rate was 13.5% versus 17% today, the new Whitehouse forecast unemployment to increase if stimulus was not passed, we were promised the automotive companies would not file bankruptcy if we bailed them out, and housing markets were forecasted to improve along with foreclosures dropping. Sadly, America has become sicker as unemployment skyrocketed, housing foreclosures hit historic highs, credit stopped flowing to consumers, commercial real estate markets teeter on collapse, the dollar is losing favor as the currency standard, and consumers curtailed their retail spending more than expected.

As individuals when our goals and plans do not work we have to reassess and change course. The most successful people consider this not a failure, but an opportunity. Watching and listening to pundits from political and financial news shows brings a plethora of analysts willing to pontificate blame. What we need is a leader; a year ago President Obama promised "Hope and Change", but today's polls show his approval rating at the lowest ever recorded for a first year president, disappointing even his most avowed supporters. I think the President's single biggest failure has not been his desires for Hope and Change, but his insistent rearview perspective of placing blame on his predecessors. Leaders do not focus on blame, instead they own their circumstances, develop responsible goals and plans, and move forward.

Our government needs to change focus now and save our society before we fall like the empires of the past. Our Founding Fathers had a radical vision for a new republic and famously changed the world with the Constitution. President Roosevelt navigated the waters of the depression with specific actionable programs. President Kennedy motivated an entire generation to put public service first and a man on the moon. Mayor Giuliani cleaned up New York City and gave its residents hope after 9/11. The consistent leadership trait among these leaders is vision and accountability.

With a new year upon us I hope our leaders in government, Obama, Reid, and Pelosi, will focus less on their political future and stop blaming those who have been gone from power for more than a year. The minority leadership can help craft a vision side by side too and the majority must understand that dissent means debate and not continue to plow forward over unanimous objection. A new year brings new opportunity and can erase thoughts of the past; I hope our government leadership, looks forward and stops looking backward.

Haiti and New Orleans (1/27/2010)

When I was 10 years old my family moved from Minnesota to California. The move was huge, but it caused me anxiety because I had watched television shows predicting the next big earthquake and California falling into the Pacific Ocean. Of course, that was more than 30 years ago, and California remains part of the continental United States. However, the residents of California live with the threat of earthquakes every day. Unlike any other natural disaster phenomena, I would conjecture an earthquake is the worst threat to face. Contrastingly, in Florida we have days, up to a week, to prepare for a hurricane. Tornadoes come with minutes of warning, or hours if paying attention to conditions. Even mudslides, floods, and fires provide a reasonable warning. An earthquake, on the other hand, comes any time and with no warning. If you live in California though, you know the threat exists. Living in Haiti on the other hand is a place with minimal earthquake risk.

Facing disaster is reasonable when you know what threat exists, or more importantly have time to prepare. When Katrina struck New Orleans warnings were issued ahead of time, the citizens had a choice to stay or leave. Of course, a weather forecast is never perfect, but with Katrina the severity of potential of the storm obviously loomed. In contrast, Haiti was struck by the worst earthquake in 200 years with no warning, and unlike California, no predisposition for the expectation of earthquakes. It appears Haiti's government and communications infrastructure collapsed, not unlike the local resources of New Orleans and Louisiana. Immediately, Haiti reached out to its neighbors to seek help, and so did New Orleans. In both instances, massive federal aid packages were mobilized to assist.

News coverage of the events in Haiti has been compassionate and focused on the successes of rescue. In South Florida the media is providing local stories of airports launching relief, medical teams departing, and families reuniting. It is nearly impossible to turn on the television without a reference to the current situation in Haiti and how the citizens of the world are reaching out to their neighbors. Unfortunately, last week there was troubling coverage of gangs, violence, and looting. I found the similarities to the aftermath of Hurricane Katrina in New Orleans striking in this regard. Sadly, there are people who disregard the brotherhood of man and instead take advantage of disaster and troubling times. Amplifying this situation is sensationalism by the press of the minority doing so. Bothersome as these situations are though, we should not be left with images of theft and violence, but focus on the success of rescue and efforts to help those in need.

However, the real story remains at the ground level, not from the massive organized efforts. The individual rescues, and thousands of examples of neighbor helping neighbor. The real survivors in Haiti are those helping, not seeking assistance or depending on a foreign nation to save the day. The real survivors understand their fate is up to them and do not blame anyone for the earthquake that struck. In contrast, the residents of New Orleans shunned personal responsibility, looked to blame others, and waited for someone to save them. Haiti's earthquake is going to forever change the look of neighboring nations as its own people realize it will take decades to recover. As we watch from afar, I challenge you to examine your own preparedness for unforeseen disasters, and remind you to believe in the goodness of people helping people.

Redux (3/3/2010)

The last few weeks I have touched on three key topics and want to revisit them today as each has made headlines, reiterating my concerns, or in one case giving hope and contradicting my thoughts. Last week I touched on energy policy, the failure of the Department of Energy to meet its mandate by President Carter, and cornucopian ignorance by conservatives. The prior week I alerted you to my concern over failing state governments. Three weeks ago I hit on the issue of entertainment and sports prevailing as the interest to Americans instead of citizenship. I typically write this column on the weekend preceding publication so it has been fascinating to watch thoughts, predictions, and trends materialize.

Snowstorms battered the mid-Atlantic and northeast again this past week reiterating my focus on state governments running budget deficits and the upcoming economic malaise. The same week I wrote my column the governors of the states met and voiced concern over impending shortfalls. In world headlines, Greece continues to make the news, but the state of California is the eighth largest economy in the world and remains on the brink of failure. On the U.S. east coast snowstorms may bankrupt individual states. For example, Georgia has no budget for snow removal but has spent $5 million. Virginia has suffered; outspending its $79 million snow removal budget by another $70 million. Those are critical monies ordinarily available for social services, schools, libraries, and road maintenance. In Virginia, the state DOT has stated all major road projects will be postponed until next fiscal year.

Thursday of last week brought the much anticipated healthcare debate. In anticipation the pundits from both the liberal and conservative views voiced excitement over the possible outcomes: would President Obama save himself and his party from defeat in 2010 or would Republicans present a concrete plan revolutionizing healthcare? Ironically with the hype to finally add transparency to the healthcare debate, most citizens will never know what took place. First, most people cannot give six hours of a weekday to watch government officials be dogmatic providing campaign like speeches. Second, the networks gave up and changed to “more interesting” programming. Thus, once again the people chose Oprah, ESPN, and daytime soap operas over engaging themselves in the strenuous process of governing America and instead will rely on media opinions and polls to persuade them.

I enjoyed writing last week’s column regarding energy policy and praising President Obama’s decision to provide loan guarantees to build two nuclear power plants in Georgia. As a follower of Peak theories, and a Chemical Engineer, I understand the mass and energy balances required to calculate the inputs required to fuel the surpluses in our society we enjoy every day. Without inexpensive fuels we would not have 2% of our society working to feed us, fertilizers and pesticides, bottled water, or cross America in a commercial jet for just $400. The ability to obtain energy cheaply provides us the lifestyle of kings; a gallon of gas bringing the energy equal to one person working nonstop for twelve weeks. Last week though, a revolutionary new fuel cell was debuted: the Bloom Box, featured on 60 Minutes, USA Today, and Forbes brings technological revolution. Ordinarily I look away, comparing such news to rainmakers invading the dustbowl in the 1930’s. However, this may be the cornucopia sought by many, a former NASA mechanical engineer has developed an ink and sand based fuel cell. The Bloom Box delivers the economic promise of powering cars and homes through a distributed network. This loaf of bread sized device may be in every home in just a few years.

What’s Happening? (4/7/2010)

The last two weeks since the passage of Obamacare have been rather odd if you follow the news closely. But it is not just Obamacare driving the craziness around us; other issues have made it to the forefront of the news which should pique interest. I did note Reid and Pelosi appear missing and the President has become the spokesman for reassuring the American people they will be cared for life now. Covered in the Washington Post Saturday was President Obama's 17-minute rambling explanation about healthcare and taxes in Charlotte, North Carolina trying to once again explain the benefits of Obamacare and why taxes must increase. Instead of trying to justify the 2,000 page Obamacare bill, the President Obama should learn from Thomas Jefferson, "*I predict future happiness for Americans if they can prevent the government from wasting the labors of the people under the pretense of taking care of them.*"

As I write this article, I am watching a news report regarding the Catholic Church. The scandal rocking the church right now is nothing new though, it is the same pedophile acts that have made news headlines in the United States. I don't understand how anyone can act surprised when it seems to be a disease of this religion, not just a new, isolated event. For example, movies have been made about past abuses and often the Priests are targets of jokes regarding children. This time, the scandal does not stop at a local Parish but appears to go to the highest ranks of the Vatican. Maybe change will come; for years it appears church members have struggled to speak out against these crimes and even now, the Church is working to stop media coverage under accusations of defamation. "All tyranny needs to gain a foothold is for people of good conscience to remain silent," Thomas Jefferson.

In the world of crazy dictators both Chavez (Venezuela) and Ahmadinejad (Iran) made the news this past week. On one hand, it's hard to take either dictator seriously, but yet they make headlines. President Chavez entertained Russia's Prime Minister Putin, met with Russian troops and spoke to them through translators. Why would these two countries build a relationship? Because Russia has technology and Venezuela has oil money. Last week the focus was a proposal for Russia to supply space and weapons technologies to Venezuela. This proposal is laughable as the country itself has energy problems, but should still be taken seriously. Chavez has increasingly built relationships with Iran, China, and Russia and worked to push himself away from the United States. Similarly, Iran's President Ahmadinejad stated he is more determined than ever to make Iran's nuclear program successful. Like a defiant child he is empowered by the threat to stop him and thus continues to aggressively pursue a nuclear weapons program. Although the United States publicly pokes fun at both countries, they continue to slowly work toward their goals and appear to achieve some success. "An enemy generally says and believes what he wishes," Thomas Jefferson.

The commonality of Ahmadinejad, Chavez, the Catholic Church, and Obama is they all believe their demagoguery. Like Jim Jones, they want the people to follow them, and to question their actions is not seen as debate but as enemies of the state. I am hopeful people around the world, and here in the United States, have awakened to the rhetoric pontificated to us. "Enlighten the people generally, and tyranny and oppressions of body and mind will vanish like evil spirits at the dawn of day," Thomas Jefferson.

Liquid Dinosaurs (5/12/2010)

This weekend we watch patiently to determine the success of the concrete containment dome being lowered onto the floor of the Gulf of Mexico to stop the oil leak. Simultaneously, coastal residents are on alert for the possibility of oil washing ashore. Sadly, our country's response has been to "keep our boot on the throat" of those they consider responsible. Ironically, we do not talk tough to those who attack our country, the religious terrorists killing our citizens, but try to destroy our friends and allies, the U.K. one of the only countries standing with us through attacks on our country.

There is a cost to retrieving liquid dinosaurs from under the earth's crust. Two weeks ago that cost was human life, but that seems forgotten now. Unlike the coal mining deaths just weeks before the families of the crew of the Deep Horizon seem forgotten. Like astronauts, these men are using technologies equivalent to going to the moon. Climbing in our SUV's, turning on the air conditioning in the Florida heat, or picking up any plastic item we take for granted the technology, costs, and lives required to recover fossil fuels. However, we are not willing to make the lifestyle change required to reduce the oil requirements.

An editorial response from a reader of USA Today this past week stated the Gulf accident is reason to move to solar, wind, and other green technologies. Unfortunately, this is the typical naïve response and overlooks how liquid fossil fuels are truly used. For perspective, each day the world consumes 86 million barrels of oil per day (3.6 billion gallons). Of that, the United States uses about 20%, or 17 million barrels. About 50% of the daily total goes toward gasoline and diesel fuel, driving our transportation infrastructure. Ultimately, automobiles and trucks, or personal transportation, can be converted to a national system of plugging in to an electrical grid. Even trains could be electrified, moving large amounts of commerce. However, aircraft will always need liquid fuels, and currently consume about 10% of the daily total. Often overlooked is the need for petroleum products to produce agricultural fertilizers, consumer plastics, and synthetic textiles. Thus, there will always be a need for liquid fossil fuels.

The Deep Horizon was an exploratory rig producing approximately 1,800 barrels per day, or 0.002% of the world's daily requirement. The well operated in 5,000 feet of water and drilling to depths of 13,000 feet – the total distance nearly three miles, or a three minute drive on the freeway. It is estimated the U.S. requirement for oil will increase by 30% over the next 20 years and in our backyard, the Gulf, there are 46 billion barrels of oil. But, before shouting "drill, baby, drill" it must be noted at current consumption rates that works out to just 2,500 days, or about eight years if that was our only oil source. We will not run out of oil, but the cost of recovery, access to, and environmental risks will continue to increase as our lives migrate to new energy sources.

Instead of playing the blame game, our government, and citizens, should be grateful for the technological skills of the engineers and scientists to continue to maintain our lifestyle. Since the early 1970's the number of tanker spills has diminished significantly. Hurricanes in the Gulf rarely cause leaks and yet these rigs float with the majesty of an Atlas rocket on the pad at Cape Canaveral. The next time someone faults an oil company for the disaster at hand, remind them of the lives lost and make sure they are not driving a car, using plastics, wearing synthetics, and eating mass produced foods. Only then do I believe they cannot be considered hypocritical.

Really? (5/19/2010)

There are days I watch the news with disbelief. Politicians offer statements and comments that my third grade son would laugh at and know are not true. Of more concern is the current the lack of experience, or just plain stupidity, of our current leaders.

Since the oil spill in the Gulf I knew jokingly George Bush would ultimately be blamed. As people would discuss the spill and what went wrong the comment would be made, "it must be George Bush's fault" and laugh about the situation. When President Obama went on the offensive, to defend his actions on Friday he placed blame for the accident squarely on the shoulders of "administrations of the past decade". I addressed such actions in prior columns and now we can conclude with certainty Obama is responsible for nothing. It appears anything, however remote to the past, will always be blamed on Bush.

There was no surprise in the media to Obama's nomination of Kagan for Supreme Court Justice. With no record of judicial experience she is as qualified as the President is for his position. Kagan's action to remove military recruiters at Harvard was unanimously overturned by the Supreme Court, and she has a failing track record arguing cases as Solicitor General. Her writings demonstrate contempt for the Constitution, and favoritism of a strong leftist approach to government. Compared to the President the only qualification she lacks is "Community Organizer."

Finally, Attorney General Eric Holder made comments that should make every American stop in their tracks and say, "huh?" As Attorney General Holder's job is to uphold the laws of the land and ensure constitutionality. Since the passage of Arizona's "Enforcement of Immigration Laws" (AZ SB1070) Holder, and Obama, have both publicly criticized the law. On Thursday Holder was questioned before Congress and stated "I grant that I have not read it…my comments are based on reading news reports, watching television." I am appalled the Attorney General and President criticize American citizens without reading legislation.

This morning I read the 17-page Arizona Bill in ten minutes. Based on the selection of Kagan for Supreme Court nominee, my ability to read state legislation, and the fact I took the LSAT I should be nominated for a high judicial position within the Obama administration. I can't wait to see what this week brings; I only know it will be George Bush's fault.

Taking Back Roads (5/26/2010)

On a recent trip from New Smyrna Beach back to North Georgia I departed the comfort and safety of the interstate highway for a back road. In this case it was Highway 341 near Brunswick, Georgia threading its way through the landscape of Jessup, Braselton, and ultimately changing roads to Dublin, Georgia. Leaving the interstate forces me to slow down, lending opportunity to look around. Gone are the Tanger Outlet malls, truck stops, and billboards. Instead, roadside stands appear, homes front the road, and Main Street comes into view. Each giving pause to what I would describe as the "real America."

The rise of interstate highway travel brought families closer together and eased the transportation of commerce. From President Eisenhower we inherited a system of roads unique to America, meant to defend our country in the cold war. However, a hidden cost of this new method of transportation came too. Like "Radiator Springs" in my 2 ½ year-old son

James' favorite movie, "Cars", towns were bypassed and left to die like withering grapes on the vine. Exiting I-95 to travel these roads requires slowing down at a town square, looking at family owned businesses in downtown, or seeing a local service station on the side of the road.

My wife and I looked with fascination at nature stealing homes and buildings. It does not take long for the weather, trees, and vines to destroy a once thriving farm or home. However, nearby structures grow, whether a modern "McMansion" or a single-wide mobile home Americans live and prosper. Instead of seeing blight I see hard-working individuals who are often mocked by Hollywood, Northeasters, Washington, and the media, but these citizens revere their God, country, and family. Towns like Lumber City, Georgia drive the economic engine of our country to deliver pine 2x4's awaiting the return of construction that may not come again. Like the Interstate that passed them by before; the politicians are now claiming successes and a "new normal" ready to pass them by again.

Our Supreme Court Bench consists of only Ivy League law graduates; Congress is 90% composed of attorneys. Instead of mocking hard-working Americans with deep-rooted values who protest an irresponsible political class spending future generations' wealth I wish our politicians would leave Washington D.C. and travel the back roads to meet the real America.

My Greatest Job (6/9/2010)

A year ago I had to quit the greatest job I ever had, teaching at Deltona High School. I remain in touch with my students, continuing to get calls, emails, text messages, and Facebook comments. Some are to tell me how they are doing; others are to ask for my help. I had over 160 students and I taught four periods of Honors Chemistry and two periods of AP Environmental Science.

Working as a teacher gave me insights I never could have imagined. Teachers spend more time with our children than most parents, they are the most important asset our country has, but as the economy has worsened teachers have become disposable targets. Now, I watch with dismay as local municipalities nationwide are struggling to meet their budgets and newspaper reports show thousands of teachers being laid off. No system is perfect, as the local contribution of property taxes first flows to the state capital and then is allocated back to the local school board by complicated formulas.

The budget consists of two parts: operating and capital, about 40% and 60% respectively. The capital budget funds buildings and debt service whereas the operating budget has sustained most of the cuts. I believe schools have focused monies incorrectly on "technology in the classroom" and buildings where hundreds of millions of dollars built new schools, rivaling the nicest hotels and office buildings. Schools now have IT departments, equivalent to dot-com companies, but have cut arts, music, and after-school sports. But, salaries and benefits make up the bulk of the operating budget and must be managed to bring the budget in line. I would focus first on top-heavy salaries and then closely examine the unionized system where longevity and mediocrity are rewarded instead of performance. Disparities of $50,000/year exist due to tenure and length of service, not quality of teaching.

Through all of these problems, I believe our local schools do an excellent job. For example, New Smyrna Beach Middle School has been an "A" rated school two years in a row and about a one-fourth of the students managed to make the Honor Roll throughout the entire year. Principals like Jim Tager navigate these times by keeping the focus on students and receiving outstanding parental support through PTA. Our future is our children and we need to protect them, not deny them the best possible teachers and education.

My Dad (6/16/2010)

My Dad turned 71 years old on May 26th. To celebrate, my wife, son, and I took my Dad and Mom to a local restaurant for wings, something he had only once before. During dinner I interrogated my Dad; asking questions about his childhood, life on the farm, school, and enlisting in the Air Force. I joked with my Dad that I knew he had no friends growing up because he did not have a Facebook page. Through all of the conversation though it reminded me how different his life was from mine, and how different the children of today are living.

My Dad was born in a farm house, not a hospital. My Grandmother did not worry about insurance; she had my Dad anyway. Living in a wooden house on 200-acres in Scandia, Minnesota the family raised crops, milking cows, pigs, and poultry. My Dad was expected to help on the farm before and after school, he had no cell phone, no computer, and did not have television until he was 14. To get to school he walked, in the snow, nearly two miles. By comparison, his grandchildren get a ride everyday in an air-conditioned car to the doorsteps of school, watch endless hours of television, have cell phones, and have minimal chores.

My Dad has lived through 13 presidencies, from Roosevelt to Obama. He has worked a variety of jobs and struggled with recessions. I cannot imagine the amount of money he has paid in taxes, well over a million dollars, and now he reaps the benefit of a broken Social Security and questionable Medicare system. Once he collected unemployment for a few weeks in the recession of 1981, but has given far more than he will ever receive.

My Dad never expected anyone to give something to him for nothing, and he taught me the same. He inspired me to work hard, be true to my word, and have integrity. My Dad worked hard to have bigger homes, new cars and "stuff". My Dad does not see life as a lottery; with some people luckier than others. Sadly, our country seems to have an opposite view where government is considered the better choice over private business, subsidizing those who choose not to work so they can have "stuff", and mocking people like my Dad for his values, integrity, and hard work.

Family (6/30/2010)

Life in North Georgia is very different than Volusia County. One noticeable difference is the number of foster families I have met. Father's Day last week made me think, "What is family?" My version of family was the 1950's Nelsons, Ozzie and Harriett, not my own family of Nelsons, although, my grandparents would have been similar in just about every aspect.

Today's kids come from many different backgrounds. In the last week I met three different people, but they all share the same thing, they have given of themselves to raise other people's kids. The first conversation was with a woman in her mid-30's who has six children. Two of the six are biological and the other four were foster children, all adopted now. Yesterday I met a man who for the last seven months has been a foster parent to a five-year old boy and his eight-year-old sister, both born to a drug addicted woman and who will forever suffer issues tied to their start in life. Last, was a 50-year-old man whose daughter was murdered by a drunk driver two years ago; he has now adopted his grandson and is raising him. A far different vision of retirement than he expected to have. Even my own children have learned to deal with divorced parents and managing two distinct homes. They have a half-brother from my remarrying and step-siblings from their mother's remarrying. Blended families bring issues, but yet we work through them.

Some kids are fortunate, or maybe not, to have a stable nuclear family. Others are thrust into circumstances we would not wish on anyone. We have an incredible society where unrelated people give of themselves to take care of other people's children. We have a disgusting society where parents will choose to selfishly indulge themselves and neglect their own children. On Father's Day I put my priority on my kids – the four people I would not trade for anything. In the following days I watched news reports with dismay as Tony Hayward of BP was criticized for taking several hours off to spend time with his son, but yet he had been discharged of his duties related to the Gulf four days earlier. Contradictorily, President Obama was given a pass to play golf, on Father's Day, for many hours absent his children. Family is what we make of it, even under pressure we have to find time to support our children first.

Carbon Copy America (8/18/2010)

My wife and I came down off the mountain this weekend and visited "civilization" to engage in the most popular sport in America: leisure shopping. Visiting the Mall of Georgia is like visiting Altamonte Mall. The similarities start with traffic lights, waiting to make turns, localized strip malls with a variety of specialty stores, car dealers using balloons to lure naïve consumers, and franchised eateries overfeeding overweight patrons. My first inclination is to shop locally, like I did in New Smyrna at Coronado Hardware or eating at the Dolphin View, but lacking choices I was forced to head to the Mall.

My intent here is not to complain about the Mall, but to comment on willfulness to trade perceived success for lost identity. I have previously written about the "good old days", circa 2006 during the boom, and also commented on the loss of small towns in my column, "Taking Back Roads." At the end of our shopping expedition on Saturday my wife, LeeAnn, said, "we could be anywhere in America. Looking around the stores and architecture are no different here or in Altamonte Springs, Ft. Worth, or Minneapolis." Her observation was spot on; we chose the economic path that brought our destruction and it started in the early 1990's. Thinking back to the 1970s and 1980s, appliance and electronics stores were locally owned; Home Depot, Lowes, and Best Buy did not exist except in their original markets. Wal-Mart was a regional Arkansas chain, not a megastore found in every town in America. Even the Mall's department stores appeared quirky to the out-of-state traveler as they represented decades old local businesses like Burdines, Daytons, Wanamakers, and Gimbels. And of course, the out parcels of Linens and Things, Old Navy, and Michaels did not exist.

In the 1990's with easy access to money, a rapidly rising stock market, low barriers to brokerage services and do-it-yourself investment attitudes the economic boom erased our identity. Local architecture and business acquiesced to national franchises and bland buildings void of character delivering mass-produced Chinese merchandise meant to symbolize success to anonymous strangers. On a local level builders nationalized and did the same, trading character for mass production of McMansions with bathrooms larger than the prior generation's living rooms. New Smyrna Beach and Cleveland, Georgia lag behind, but yet both claim progress by advancing box stores and abandoning local business heritage. Just push "Copy", America has lost her character.

Gender Bias (8/25/2010)

Last week I encountered a woman I previously knew; a very attractive successful vice president of a national company. Ironically, her reputation is one of being a "total b—ch". This prompted me to wonder why people feel intimidated by successful women whereas I have always been attracted to and admired successful intelligent women. Personally, my wife LeeAnn is beautiful, has worked as a financial controller for a Ross Perot company with numerous people reporting to her, and is now attaining her CPA. Similarly, my girlfriend prior to LeeAnn turned heads and is vice president of a national healthcare company. But yet, both are denigrated by people who do not know them. Having two daughters I feel hypersensitive to this issue as I encourage and push them to achieve more, challenging them academically. However, their friends, and even some family, fail to support and push them.

Sadly, it appears many Americans regard successful, attractive women as enemies; often denigrated with the "b" or "c" words. A woman relegated to part-time work or a stereotypical female job finds herself held in higher regard, but it seems these women are the first to insult those who have found success. Among males, the opposite is true. A tough, good looking guy rising to a top-management position, becoming a politician or powerful lawyer is admired.

Examples of tough women at leadership levels abound from Pelosi and Palin, Secretary of State Clinton, Germany's Merkel, England's former Thatcher, and even our own local Suzanne Kosmas and Dorothy Hukill. These are the women I use as role models for my daughters, the ladies who have proven with hard work and determination, regardless of gender, they can rise and chase dreams. Unfortunately, more Americans uphold Lohan, Spears, and Snooki. It appears there is more regard for pop stars void of opinion and intellect, lacking morals, values, and ethics, but high on scandal, promiscuity, and even criminal activity. Successful women find themselves mocked and maligned, like Sarah Palin. What woman serves as a better role model than Palin, who spoke out locally, rose through the ranks and became governor and the second female vice presidential candidate in American history? It's easy to disparage people we don't know, calling them trailer trash, a b—ch, or reference lipstick on a pig. If dislike is driven by disagreement over issues, then debate, but don't make it personal.

The Twilight Zone (11/17/2010)

My buddy Noel and I were talking this week about the rising cost of fuel, unemployment, President Obama's actions in Asia, rising gold prices, crashing housing prices, and "Dancing with the Stars". I said it felt like we were in the "The Twilight Zone". You see, Noel and I are the same age as each other, born in 1967. I commented that we grew up with Gene Cernan hitting golf balls on the moon and promises of us living there someday.

We were influenced by TV re-runs like "The Brady Bunch", "Leave it to Beaver", and "Andy Griffith". The 1970's had the gas crunch, Nixon going to China, the Bicentennial, Jimmy Carter, and the Iranian Hostage crisis. As we entered high school Reagan protected us from the Soviets, and the Big 3 auto companies saved themselves from the Japanese. In college Bush 1 continued the legacy of Reagan and we graduated to a healthy job market. Clinton first scared us with Hillarycare and reinvented himself to ultimately steer a healthy economy where everyone talked dotcoms, and knew Peter Lynch's name; investment returns less than 15% were despised. Even as we partied like it was 1999, life remained good, our careers flourished, and although terrorism was new to our shores, we all jumped on the real estate rocket ship.

Today I feel like a character in the Twilight Zone: I lost my job, like Donald Trump sold real estate at a loss, shed assets like "The Biggest Loser", have watched two elections with dismay wondering how some get reelected and others lost, and been puzzled by the bank mess and healthcare. On television gay characters perpetuate, obesity delights, and sitcom dialogue offends. I used to love air travel, but George Bush created a Gestapo security force requiring me to show papers, remove my shoes, and in the latest round choose radiation or molestation to board a plane. My president claims Islam was the light of the world, but yet the followers of this political radicalism have killed over 3,100 Americans in the last decade, many on our own soil. America manufactures nothing, we regurgitate services, and our economy is fueled by debt and consumption; there are no jobs and it will take 20 years to recover the 8 million lost over the last three years. Last week the central bank announced it will print money until our economy is fixed, another crazy scheme parallel to the Fed's efforts of the Great Depression. My only explanation is we are waiting for Rod Serling to step from behind a tree saying, "That's the signpost up ahead – your next stop, The Twilight Zone!"

My Buddy Neil (1/26/2011)

My buddy Neil is a great guy and well entrenched in his opinions as he is in his mid-70's. One topic which always leads to vigorous, friendly disagreement is politics; as a senior citizen Neil enjoys and takes advantage of many of the programs offered him, like Medicare and Social Security. Overall, he feels entitled to benefits available to someone like him who worked hard all his life. I guess I can't blame him, but I grew up being told social security would not exist when I needed it. In fact, it is now broke and taking in less money than payouts. Sadly, the government "borrowed" against the Social Security trust fund and there is nothing but journal entries reflecting what should be a solid program.

Meanwhile I, in my mid 40's, feel like I carry the world on my back to produce and earn income, not only for my own family, but due to taxes for many other people too. Neil and I have conflict on what we see as the role of government. Last week we discussed politics: Obama, Fox News, Democrats and Republicans. In the course of conversation Neil commented he didn't realize I write this column every week, thinking I was an occasional guest appearance. He challenged me, wondering about my position and I explained I try to hold a middle ground and this earned a respectable smile.

I quickly reminded him I don't have cable television and therefore the opinions I write are original. He asked how I see the world, "left or right?" I replied I have realized during the last 70 columns I am a libertarian and my friend's eyes opened wide whilst asking me to define myself further. Suddenly I found myself defending what I would call the anarchists view of libertarian politics. Instead, I explained my definition of libertarianism is quite easy, "we need nothing more than 7 of the 10 commandments and they serve as a guidebook for libertarianism." In short, in the middle, I believe less government is good; I can make better decisions than anyone else can on my behalf, and we should not legislate against stupidity. As the "Man in the Middle" I try hard weekly to maintain a balance and offer original opinions and insights. By the way I sent Neil my last 70 columns and look forward to debating what he reads.

Left – I agree more than you think (3/2/2011)

I rarely read the columns to my Left and Right on this page, but recently was made aware of a comment asserting I had a "Right" bias. Although probably not far off at first glance, due to my fear of tyranny through larger government, I thought I might take on the challenge and clarify many of my positions for all who read. I compiled a list of my columns for the last 80 weeks and saw a common theme emerging, one that distances me from most on the Right and those on the Left, but more so defining a tolerant middle-ground. Let me proceed.

We should not have a death penalty, in my opinion to put one innocent man to death is far more grievous an error than all the guilty men "legally" killed. In contrast I would argue the same applies to abortion and we should not terminate those who cannot speak for themselves. I do not support school sponsored prayer, or even prayer at a public event. At the same time I feel it is wrong to tell someone they cannot pray or express themselves religiously, both positions fail to respect the individual. I do believe the environment should be protected at all costs, to not be a conservationist is only destroying the world for future generations. However I am of the opinion Global Warming is complete hogwash. Regarding healthcare, as dutiful men we need to care for the indigent and infirmed, but government is least likely the right mechanism to transfer such wealth whereas charity and selflessness will more efficiently provide.

I move far from the left on the concept of income redistribution and sincerely believe all men are created equal, and therefore have an equal chance of success. However, I do believe some amount of government regulation is necessary as many men will choose cheating and scheming over honesty.

Like many on the Left I believe the Patriot Act was the most abusive attack on our civil rights ever made and it should be immediately abolished. Unlike those on the Left I believe the Founding Fathers did not see the Constitution as a living document, fearing tyranny, and wanted to give liberty from government to future generations.

I can state my position succinctly: I love my country, but fear my government. "When the people fear their government, there is tyranny; when the government fears the people, there is liberty." - Thomas Jefferson.

Higher Education Myth (7/6/2011)

My daughter is 15, just finished her freshman year of high school. Like many parents with a high school student I am carefully watching her grades and doing everything I can to ensure she will make it to college. Over the last four decades the number of students going to college has increased, and so have the costs. I was the first in my family to attend college, earning my way on a scholarship and understanding the path in front of me: attend school, work hard, get good grades, and graduate expecting to find a good paying job. Even in the 1980s I was puzzled by the choice of major some would make, possibly liberal arts related and then wonder why they could not find a job. As an Engineer I was showered with job offers and an excellent starting salary (nearly $39,000 in 1990).

Today it appears college has become an entitlement program, fueled by readily available public financing and a willing consumer unqualified to receive a "real education." In 2011 the average public university cost will be $20,000 per year, and a private school twice that much. Assume your son or daughter is following their passion into liberal arts and a 4-year degree will approach $160,000 with income prospects of $25-30,000 per year; if they are lucky. Sadly, there is an assumption these students are qualified for education, and more so entitled to a job at graduation. I recently heard this anecdote, "Just because you have fishing license does not mean you know how to catch a fish, or will catch a fish. College degrees are the same, a piece of sheepskin will not guarantee success."

College debt in America is now $800 billion and less than 54% of graduates in 2010 were able to find work. The Washington Post reported 85% of college graduates will be returning home. As a father, I must weigh what advice I would give my children and truly wonder, unless tuition is covered by a scholarship, whether college is worth the liability (note, I did not say investment) created. Like the housing crisis and shoddy loans, college degrees are being handed out to unqualified and undeserving students with no prospects of work, but fully guaranteed by the U.S. taxpayer. We must remember a fishing license will not cause fish to jump in the boat, nor will a college degree cause paychecks to fall from the sky.

My 100th Column (07/27/2011)

This week I celebrate my 100th column, a huge milestone for me as I could not have imagined writing for "The Observer" for nearly two years without missing a week; I just wish my high school English teacher could see me now. I want to thank the publishers for the opportunity, seeing something they liked and allowing me free reign to pontificate as I desire. It was freelance writing, "Death and Taxes" that won me the opportunity and I find it ironic it is that issue, taxes, currently in front of the American people. As I look back over the last 99 weeks I note my philosophies have emerged where I feel I can clearly define my views: libertarian (with a little "L"), constitutionalist fearful of eroding liberties, and angry at politicians feeling anointed to spend, steal, and create laws but yet hold themselves above the people.

My early columns could be republished today: "What is Government's Role", "When Should Citizens Fear their Government?", and "Big Brother is Watching." Sadly I look back and see a country that has worsened during the last 100 weeks and continues to spin into the abyss while the citizenry look the other way to take in meaningless hype like Casey Anthony, the NFL, and "Dancing with Stars." Two forces have united to provide the Kool-Aid for apathy, the media and the President. Right now we are two years into the economic recovery: remember "Green Shoots", Biden and Obama touting all of the jobs they saved, and the National Realtors Association calling the bottom to housing prices? This deception is dutifully reported by the three networks and bull-horned by General Electric owned MSNBC and CNBC.

Over the weekend, the networks gave more time to the Amy Winehouse drug-induced death than the critical issues. Did you know last week gold hit a historic high over $1,600/ounce; jobless claims topped 400,000 for the 15th week in a row; and Borders (closed 399 stores), Cisco and Lockheed Martin announced combined layoffs of 23,000? Since January state and local governments have laid off 142,000 workers. Let's not forget last week's media celebration of American Airlines ordering jets from Airbus, a consortium of European companies, a staggering loss to domestic aircraft producers. Although our President tells us things are better and improving it is impossible to conclude the same when looking at the numbers. Likewise the 1930s were a long road of government missteps trying to fix problems created by the same banking cartel whose lineage has brought the same destruction upon us today. Looking back, history provides hilarious quotes from our leaders during the Great Depression trumpeting the recovery and "Happy Days are Here Again." I believe Obama and Biden will be similarly chided for their mistruths when history is chiseled.

3 GOVERNMENT

When Should Citizens Fear Their Government? (11/4/2009)

I recently bought a bumper sticker, "I love my country, but fear my government". With shocking reality I realized I have more in common with the granola-eating, hemp-wearing, Volvo-driving hippies of the 1960's counterculture than I do with the citizen conformists I thought I was like. The First Amendment guarantees our right to associate and assemble freely. However, I believe our government is now taking steps to significantly erode this freedom, among other civil liberties, at all levels, federal, state, and local.

Naomi Wolfe, author of "The End of America," makes a compelling case for fascist America as she compares the Bush Administration's "War on Terror" actions and passing of various legislative pieces to the dictatorships in 1930's Europe. Personally, I have always been bothered by "The Department of Homeland Security", domestic wiretapping and surveillance laws, and the overreaching methods of TSA at airports. I had a letter published in another newspaper about the "SS" like methods in use following 9/11 and thereafter found myself on TSA's watch list. This seemed like more than a coincidence to me. Vigilance is important, but giving up liberties for the perception of safety is the biggest mistake anyone society can make.

In October 2008, for the first time ever, the United States Army stationed troops domestically. The guise of this deployment is to provide a federal response to assist with disasters, terrorism, and crowd control. During Katrina, the private security force "Blackwater" was enlisted to police and enforce martial law. Blackwater has forces stationed at the headwaters to the Great Lakes and on the California border. Each state allows the Governor to call on the National Guard to assist with disasters, or more importantly enforce martial law. In all of these instances our citizenry is allowing civil rights to erode in the name of perceived safety. Do you trust Blackwater?

When the G20 met in Pittsburgh my concern was raised again. Local police in battle regalia carried military assault weapons to use against American citizens. Of more concern Pittsburgh police used an audio cannon manufactured by American Technology Corporation, a San Diego-based company, to disperse protesters outside the G-20 Summit , the first time its LRAD series device has been used on civilians in the U.S. This weapon is funded to local police departments nationwide by grants from the Department of Homeland Security; thus there is no record of which police departments are in possession of this weapon, what training they have undergone, or ability to monitor their plans to deploy these weapons.

With the H1N1 virus creating an atmosphere of unknown possible outbreaks states have seized the opportunity to modify legislation to create quarantines, martial law, take property, and criminalize failure to follow department of health orders; Massachusetts' Senate approved bill S.2028 (Pandemic Response Bill) is the most appalling example. Nationally, police and military have trained for roadside checkpoints, and the city of Boston has tested an RDIF tracking system for vaccinations. In October police chiefs endorsed spying on neighbors and the Department of Homeland Security and FBI issued circulars to business owners alerting them to watch for possible purchases of certain chemicals and report these purchases as possible terrorism.

Regardless of political view, the erosion of our civil liberties from both sides of the aisle and all levels of government is obvious. Slowly, we are becoming like the countries of Eastern Europe. Am I the only one that sees this resemblance? Sadly, we appear to be willingly giving up our civil liberties in the name of safety.

Constitutional Charity (11/18/2009)

I received feedback on the column I wrote, "Death and Taxes," in September. Overall the reader agreed with my position, but found herself bothered by my lack of compassion for needy people. In the column I argued we do everything we can to avoid death, but not to avoid taxes. I accept we need to pay taxes to the extent we need to support a civilized society, but I take issue with tax collection for other purposes that are non-essential.

She said we have a duty to "take care of those in need" and this position was prompted by her values. I certainly agree with the desire and need to take care of others, and personally I have given time and money to charitable causes. This issue has always seemed to be a bone of contention between people with one side appearing to lack any compassion and the other giving away everything with no concern for consequences. However, I know I am not without compassion and through my actions I know I help those in need. But, I believe this should be done through charity and is not a role of government.

Fortunately, I believe I found the clarity to express my thoughts better; several weeks ago I read a weekly column by writer Frank Miele of the "Daily Inter Lake" in Kalispell, Montana. In his column, he used the historical example of Davey Crockett, the three-term Congressman from Tennessee in the 1820s who found himself confronted by an angry constituent, Horatio Bunce, about Crockett's recent vote for a bill to provide $20,000 of federal funds fire victims ravaged and left homeless in nearby Georgetown. Crockett was asked, "Where do you find in the Constitution any authority to give away the public money in charity?" Like most of us, Crockett gave a list of reasons about helping others and doing the right thing, giving charity.

"You gave a vote last winter which shows that either you have not capacity to understand the Constitution, or that you are wanting in the honesty and firmness to be guided by it. In either case you are not the man to represent me," Bunce said. Upon review, it is obvious, the founding fathers made no accommodation for a constitutional authority of the government to transfer the wealth of one citizen to another through the process of taxation. Modern examples of this would be hurricanes and wildfires. Of course, other more questionable examples abound such as "Cash for Clunkers", first-time home buyer subsidies, funding shortfalls to the New York unemployment fund, the health insurance reform proposals, and any other federal program providing direct payments and transfers of wealth from one group of citizens to another

This past summer Tea Parties made headlines, unfortunately they were sensationalized for many wrong reasons. The idea for the Tea Parties was spurned by Rick Santelli on CNBC when he editorialized in outrage over the proposals for government stimulus programs. This outrage was not due to lack of compassion for those in need or lack of concern for America and the economy. It was outrage over the reach of government into individual wealth, no matter how big or small, and the desire to take it and transfer it to others.

Like Davey Crockett I struggle with my personal since of compassion versus constitutional intent. We have a strong document that was meant to create a sound democracy for centuries. Every time it is "interpreted", ignored, and eroded for social purposes we take away our own liberties and freedoms.

Not True (2/3/2010)

Middle ground is often hard to find, regardless of whether you try to get there from the left or the right. President Obama made the news three times last week, with each appearance being overshadowed more by politics than the substance behind his comments. His presidency has taken the appearance of a rudderless ship, using the press and public opinion to drive short term goals with no strategic plan to maintain direction. Weekly the administration's cast of characters marches onto the Sunday morning talk shows and Emanuel, Axelrod, Gibbs, and even Clinton pontificate this week's new agenda. Like the Clinton years, weekly trial balloons are floated and the Chicago political machine drives the weekly agenda. Sadly, the theme of the week does not deliver substance, but instead takes our country on "Mr. Toad's Wild Ride".

A historic opportunity was in front of President Obama last week with the State of the Union Address. However, he again shifted blame for the economy back to the prior eight years before he was elected; offering a repeated argument, he "inherited a failing economy after eight years of bad decisions." I have previously offered that leaders need to own situations, plans, and provide concrete strategies, but Obama prefers to savor projecting blame. Worsening his image, his speech was overshadowed by his gaffe against the Supreme Court's recent first amendment ruling. He erred in stating foreign corporations would be allowed to spend in our elections, although 2 U.S.C. 441e(b)(3) prevents this and Justice Alito responded, forever tainting the tone of the speech.

On Friday Obama went to Baltimore to dialogue directly with the Republican Caucus. News reports showed sparring, and the "Huffington Post" reported he mauled the lions in the lion's den. A frequent video clip of the networks is Obama stating, "I am not an ideologue." However, my check of the dictionary shows an ideologue to be "an often blindly partisan advocate or adherent of a particular ideology." My recollection of the last twelve months is locking the minority party out of discussions on health care, mocking the passionate citizens of the minority, and demonizing anyone who disagrees with the majority's agenda. Regardless, I am impressed he engaged, and more importantly did so without a teleprompter.

Saturday was much more in line with the sound bites this President enjoys. His appearance on the sidelines and participating in the commentary at the Georgetown vs. Duke basketball game drove home his likeability. Comfortable in the celebrity style spotlight and ravishing the attention, Obama delivered his typical one-liner partisan dig when asked about being left-handed and responded, "I went to the Republican House caucus just yesterday to prove that I could go to my right once in a while." Once again though, he received significant coverage of an insignificant event, managing his image and failing to deliver substance.

This last week shined light on the tissue paper thin qualifications of our President and peeled the onion back to show a man that continues to operate in campaign mode, not a strong leader with the strength he promised. The State of the Union a year later was the platform to recount "Hope and Change". However, promises were broken – Guantanamo, Afghanistan, reducing unemployment – all of which don't require opposition party support. Even ramming the largest healthcare bill in history into the economy was not accomplished because he cannot lead his own party. Last week's State of the Union speech could have enticed all Americans, but the populist platform rang hollow with disappointment.

Energy Policy (2/24/2010)

America's energy policy over the last 40 years has been lacking direction, but President Obama took a big step forward last week. Prior to 1972 America was an exporter of oil, not only supplying all of our own needs but exporting oil to other countries. It is hard to imagine, but in the early 20th century oil literally flowed to the top of the ground in places like

Pennsylvania, no wells, no deep sea drilling; it could be had by scraping it off the ground. In 1956 a geophysicist, Dr. M. King Hubbert predicted by 1970 America would reach its "peak", the point where U.S. oil production would peak. However, the concept of "Peak Oil" is scoffed at since we continue to discover more oil reserves, dismissing that every new barrel costs more to obtain than the previous. In 1973 the OPEC crisis catalyzed our country's quest for energy independence; seven presidents since influenced America's energy policies, but yet we remain hostage to foreign sources.

In 1977 President Carter created the Department of Energy; a bloated bureaucracy failing to meet its original mandate. Specifically, the DOE was created to ensure "the U.S. will never again import as much oil as it did in 1977." At its creation, America imported 8.6 million bbls/day, now we import 10.4 million bbls/day. The DOE has grown from zero employees and zero budget to over 16,000 taxpayer paid civil servants, 100,000 contractors and an annual budget of $28 billion. Today America remains as dependent on foreign sources of energy as in 1977. Contrastingly, President Reagan brought a different view to office regarding energy. Sadly, his view is one that has stayed with Republicans during the last 25 years. Regan, a cornucopian, believed an innovative, technological solution, would appear in time to save us from the tragedy of our misdeeds. Of course, President Reagan, and his British counterpart Margaret Thatcher, were saved by the huge North Sea oil discoveries in the 1980s. Thus, the UK had a thriving economy and postponed energy policy decisions and likewise America did the same.

In the summer of 2008 every American received a wake-up call to energy policy. Stunned, we watched the price of gasoline at the pump soar past $4.00/gallon, considered buying "Smart" cars and left the SUV in the garage. Of course, this brought out the charlatans and snake-oil salesmen seeking government monies and investors for wind farms, off-shore wave generators, battery powered cars, oil sands recovery, and the now famous food-for-fuel, or ethanol disaster. However, grabbing a calculator and doing some math will show many of these methods require more energy than produced, do more environmental damage, or are just silly when considering large-scale implementation.

This past week President Obama made an excellent decision regarding energy policy; announcing $8.3 billion in loan guarantees to build two nuclear reactors in Georgia, the first in the U.S. in 30 years. Ironically, it is a decision that defies his party's typical philosophy regarding nuclear energy and I am certain the likes of Jane Fonda, and the rest of the anti-nuke crowd, are troubled by this. However, the Hollywood crowd driving Toyota Prius automobiles must understand their energy requirements will come from the "grid". President Obama, as a Senator and candidate, has consistently supported nuclear power. I would suggest the President add geo-thermal energy to the quest for clean-energy independence. With the unspent stimulus monies President Obama could focus a moonwalk like quest on energy and lead us out of recession and away from dependence on our enemies in the middle-east and South America.

Politics and Science (3/24/2010)

Throughout history major corporations, governments, and philanthropists have played a role in funding scientific research. Funding is required to pay salaries, buy materials, and ultimately sustain research; therefore it is reasonable to expect the funding of research to be driven by self-interest. My favorite example would be the story of Archimedes discovering the concept of density to confirm King Hiero had been swindled in making his gold crown. The outcome of his research confirmed King Hiero's concerns, and history benefitted from the discovery of the principle of density. We should be concerned when subjectivity in science overrules objectivity. The scientific method clearly outlines the objective process for creating a hypothesis, testing, analyzing data, and making valid conclusions.

I worked as an engineer, have a minor in mathematics, and am an expert in statistics, thus I believe I am well qualified to look at a set of data and make conclusions using experience and knowledge. However, I am not an expert in every field, nor is anyone. Therefore, I trust scientists to objectively examine data and come to valid conclusions. Under review, publishing, a peer process exists to monitor the scientific community. However, concern arises when this process is called into question and therefore raises doubts about conclusions and recommendations. If the conclusions are used to effect public policy the method and authorities providing the information must be trustworthy and verifiable. This past winter two issues have made the headlines illustrating my concern over politics and science.

In December there was much ado regarding the Copenhagen meetings on climate change. Although no agreement was reached, world leaders continue to create new policies to limit carbon emissions. "Global Warming" as promoted by Al Gore has always been called into question by big business. Personally, I am open to the subject of "Climate Change", but feel man's influence is insignificant when compared to Earth's Eonic existence. The scandal surrounding the global warming science forces wonder whether in this case, science was created to promote a certain agenda, manipulate data, squash contradictory views, and intimidate critics. Many have argued to require more analysis of the climate change data because there are so many variables in play to tax an entire population for a normally occurring climate trend would make no sense.

In the second case, announcements were made to change the recommended mammogram screening guidelines for women. Initially these guidelines were established to ensure early detection of breast cancer. However, the recommendation came to wait longer before beginning screenings and to lessen the frequency of screenings. Many women were outraged and examples came forth where saved lives could only be attributed to early screenings under the former guidelines. The science behind the guideline recommendations may not have been scrutinized in such detail though if public debate over health care, threats of rationing, and cutbacks in services were not in the political forefront. Thus, regardless of the possible validity of the change in recommendations to eliminate unnecessary screenings, they are tainted by politics.

We have all joked regarding a medical recommendation made one year and then overturned several years later due to new findings. It is critical that we trust scientists to maintain the ethical line between politics and science, regardless of their desire to promote a personal agenda. The scientific process is the essential first step in maintaining trust between the public and policy based on science.

Lame (Duck) (6/23/2010)

A Lame Duck is an elected official approaching the end of his tenure, thus making him ineffective. Recent articles in the *Wall Street Journal*, *US News and World Report*, and even Germany's *Der Spiegel* are comparing the President to one-term President Carter. Criticism has been flowing from his staunchest supporters such as MSNBC's Keith Olbermann and Chris Matthews. The common theme among all observers is the inability of the president to handle the problems confronting him and to stop shifting blame for his situation back to the prior administration.

Every administration in history has inherited problems; President Ford was a stop-gap president between Nixon and Carter. Throughout Carter's presidency he used the problems of President Nixon, the energy crisis, recession, and of course Watergate, to make himself appear more presidential. The hostage taking in Tehran occurred on his watch, and ultimately became his death nail when he proved he lacked the faculties to resolve the crisis.

President George HW Bush became a one-term president after bipartisan efforts to negotiate a budget resulted in reneging on a famous campaign promise, "read my lips, no new taxes." Regardless of his successful foreign policy efforts and management of the world stage, the American people were unforgiving and mandated change through a resounding defeat.

Similarly, President Obama offered "Hope and Change", but has delivered on little of what he promised. After an elegant campaign two years ago we watch with dismay wishing Hillary Clinton had won the nomination instead. Among both sides there is acknowledgment that she has proven herself loyal and demonstrated leadership characteristics. Vice President Biden correctly prophesied the President would be tested, and the fury of examinations have come both domestically and internationally: Ft. Hood, The Underwear Bomber, Times Square bombing, losing the Chicago Olympics, failing to close Guantanamo, breaking Afghanistan troop withdrawal promises, economic instability, cloudy transparency, the Gulf crisis, and a cast of Czars to guide him.

The inexperienced man, with no executive experience, has missed multiple opportunities to provide "Hope and Change." Last week was the ultimate example during the Gulf Spill speech, no solutions were offered, no Presidential analysis was given. Instead, Chicago-style political thuggery was the theme to pressure BP, ensure constituency votes were purchased, and springboard non-related legislation. We have 29 months until the next election, and I believe we have a Lame Duck president who, like President Ford, will be remembered for his golf game.

Sleeping Dogs (9/22/2010)

My dog loves to sleep, he is content having me care for him and returns the favor of unquestionable loyalty to me, watching my home, and protecting my children. However, if he were kicked while sleeping he would awake with a vengeance, ready to attack. I believe the American people, regardless of political affiliation, are like my dog: content, apathetic, happy to be cared for, and quite loyal. But something has changed during the last two years; the 300 million of us have been kicked by the 535 members of Congress and are awake, growling, and ready to attack. We are tired of the politicians in Washington stealing our futures, committing crimes, and believing they are anointed for life to govern us.

Over the last 18 months the elite political establishments have criticized the Tea Party; claiming it was orchestrated by wealthy individuals as "Astroturf." It was hypothesized it was an organized effort and no one believed the American people would come together April 15 with 750 rallies across America proving it is a grassroots effort. The major news networks incorrectly reported the movement as racist, radical right-wingers, and a split in the Republican Party. Many see this is as a grab for conservatives; so continues Washington's and the elite political establishment's misunderstanding of those they govern. I assert the Tea Party movement is America: rural and suburban people, family oriented, hard-working with morals, values and ethics. We understand Congress has passed laws over our objections, exempted itself from those laws, and stolen the future of many generations.

In the primaries last week Tea Party candidates succeeded in changing the status quo. Since April 2009 Tea Party rallies have proven they represent everyone, although portrayed as radical and racist, and even a fad, by the mainstream media. I have watched black, white, Hispanic, women and men marching together to remind Washington they need to hear us. Voter revolutions have occurred before, most notably 1994 was the last time and there was talk of term limits and strong anti-incumbent sentiment. The following years were better for all, debate was forced into the two party system, and a President with an out-of-touch agenda was forced to curtail his radical desires. The single party majority currently controlling the Congress and the Executive Branch of government has kicked the dog, forcing him to realize tyranny comes while sleeping.

Election Season – Part I (9/29/2010)

This is the first of a series I am writing in anticipation of the upcoming elections in November. Last week I commented the American people, the sleeping dogs, have been awakened. Many put their confidence in the poetry of "Change and Hope", but the prose delivered has fallen short of their romanticized expectations. Leadership and management are learned skills, not certainties due to position, advisors, charisma, or teleprompters. Blame on both parties, the elites, and the constituencies has been tossed about. Regardless of where blame falls, our country is in trouble.

In a recent discussion with my friend Monil, he brought to my attention a writing of Thomas Jefferson to Edmund Pendleton on August 26, 1776 where he wrote, "So much for the wisdom of the Senate. To make them independent, I had proposed that they should hold their places for nine years, and then go out (one third every three years) and be incapable forever of being re-elected to that house. My idea was that if they might be re-elected, they would be casting their eyes forward to the period of election (however distant) and be currying favor with the electors, and consequently dependent on them. My reason for fixing them in office for a term of years rather than for life, was that they might have an idea that they were at a certain period to return into the mass of the people and become the governed instead of the governors which might still keep alive that regard to the public good that otherwise they might perhaps be induced by their independence to forget."

Today our politicians see themselves as elites sent to Washington for life, to live off our efforts. Our two party system has ironically become a spectacle of like-minded aristocrats benefitting from larger government, more laws, and dependent constituencies. Political life at the Federal level is about personal benefit, not public service. As the election season comes upon us this year, our votes are about both our short-term future and the long-term vision for America, the future we will give our children. We watched the giddiness of a single majority manipulate parliamentary rules, object to debate, lash out at voters, run from town hall meetings, and fundamentally change our country. Whether change was best, you must decide and I challenge you to engage in the electoral process.

Election Season – Part II (10/6/2010)

Last week I challenged the reader to consider what path our country should take for the short term issues and for the long-term future we give to our children. Thomas Jefferson asserted those who govern us should be governed by the same laws and not become corrupt. In this week's preparation for Election Day I want to explore commonly used terms: liberal, conservative, and libertarian. Next week I will explore the platforms of the three parties, history, and my predictions. Labels are thrown around to negatively portray a thought process by the other side. Democrats are "liberals", Republicans are "conservatives", and Glenn Beck famously accuses both being "progressives". I must wonder where the truth lies and what each means.

Classic liberalism was at the root of the American Revolution, justifying the overthrow of tyrannical governments by focusing on individual liberty and civil rights. The philosophies of John Maynard Keynes in response to the depression created modern liberalism; arguing that in hard times free markets were not ideal and investment and intervention by the state was required. Liberalism has changed over time and across cultures since the 17th century, but at its root is a commitment to understanding humanity and society with a great degree of intellectual work to justify and validate the theories.

Conservatism is most likely the most incorrectly applied label, and should be defined as seeking to preserve traditional institutions and maintain gradual changes in society. Unlike liberalism, conservatism was not spawned by intellectual goals and improvements, but came from preservation, emphasizing stability and continuity. The modern application comes from the split in views in the 1930s and Keynesian economics.

Libertarianism more closely represents today's incorrect definition of conservatism; the view that each person has the right to live his life freely, but respecting the equal rights of others. Libertarians believe all actions should be voluntary, with only the most basic tenets of life forbidden by law.

The term "progressive" was coined at the start of the 20th century and focused on driving an agenda of change. Correctly, progressivism and conservatism are antonyms of each other. In our modern political environment we have three philosophies: modern liberalism, classic liberalism, and libertarianism where the rate of change is defined by terms progressivism and conservatism. Carefully consider what you claim to be and where your views lie, more carefully consider the labels you apply to others.

Election Season – Part III (10/13/2010)

In last week's column I worked to explore the definitions of the labels so quickly applied to describe various political views: liberal, conservative, and libertarian. Talk radio pundits regularly throw labels around with the intent of degrading the reputation of someone merely by association. This week I want to examine the platforms of the two major parties and the rising Tea Party movement. I believe many people hear the labels and the names of the parties, but do not understand the history, or more importantly the platform. Today candidates are changing, or leaving parties, like grabbing flip-flops for the beach so I must wonder how important are the parties?

Liberalism is the renowned platform of the Democrats, essentially incorporating Progressivism to drive a humanitarian agenda based on intellectual theory and conjecture. The last 80 years have used Keynesian economics to justify government programs as the solution to capitalistic shortfalls. Thus, the Democrats are seen as a champion of the lower class, providing social protections. Democrats evolved from anti-federalist factions in the 1790's and today represent the single largest political party in the world. The Party once favored states rights and strict adherence to the constitution. Today the Party favors liberalism, social not classical, and has embraced Clinton's "Third Way" , believing government should play a role in alleviating poverty and social injustice and use a system of progressive taxation to implement policy.

Conservatism is used to describe Republicans, having evolved from Classic Liberalism, originally focusing on individual rights and civil liberties. This pre-1930's attitude drives a platform allowing the individual to excel but forcing him to deal with the consequences of his own decisions. The Republican Party was founded in 1854 by anti-slavery activists and saw Abraham Lincoln as its first president. By the 1890's the Party was known for protecting business, primarily through tariffs, the gold standard, and high wages. The Party also opposed the League of Nations. Today, Republicans are defined by social-conservatism, supply-side economics, support for gun ownership, and deregulatory policies.

The newly formed Tea Party is a populist movement in response to Congressional Bills passed in 2009. The Tea Party's platform is focused on ensuring the constitutionality of every law, fiscal responsibility, limiting federal spending, reducing earmarks and reducing taxes. Although new, the Tea Party has demonstrated its ability to put forth viable, electable candidates and has forced the two traditional parties to defend their positions in political debate.

Election Season – Part IV (10/20/2010)

Over the last three weeks I have tried to address basic political issues regarding the platforms of the two major parties and the labels applied to describe agendas. With a major election less than two weeks away it is important to understand how the political system works. I feel the 2008 election is an excellent example of our constitutional right to vote where the casual voters caused a "mandate by the American people," now about to be overturned in another mandate this fall after watching vote selling, favoritism, and power abuse by the majority.

Unfortunately, media attention typically centers on national politics, many people unable to name the President, fewer able to name the Vice President, Speaker of the House, or Senate Majority Leader. These people drive the national agenda and play a significant role in our lives. For instance, national healthcare has been passed and Congress has eliminated incandescent light bulbs; decisions driven on the national level. I argue our state, county, and city elections take as much priority as the national elections though, but too many people scoff at these politics.

Unnoticed, the School Board influences local property tax values and potentially sales tax rates. With our school district, county, and cities in financial dire straits it is critical we understand our local candidates and their fiscal policies because two approaches exist to balancing budgets: cutting expenses or increasing tax revenues. At all local levels of government the millage rate can increase; an easier decision than cutting services, salaries, and pensions. Our local politicians can increase taxes with a vote of four out of seven members, thus just one person can create thousands of dollars in increased annual expenses for your family.

Even Volusia County's Elections Supervisor found herself at the center of national attention during the Gore-Bush Presidential election of 2000 when voting recounts became critical, certifying election results under the scrutiny of the national media. Few of us realize the members of the Canvassing Board came from our locally elected judges, ultimately deciding the Presidential Election. Proposed amendments are more important as they will ultimately impact policy, tax rates, and budgets for years to come. Proposals like Amendment 4, Hometown Democracy, have the potential to destroy the normal legislative process, relying instead on the populace to make ill-informed decisions argued at the ballot. I urge you to study and learn about your ballot before November 2nd.

Election Season – Part V (10/27/2010)

Most American voters are stupid, but you are different because you are reading this column, this page, and this paper. Unfortunately, everyone else seems to wait for someone to tell them what to do and how to vote, whether it's by the constant barrage of political attack ads or the non-stop voices of Hannity, Limbaugh, Olbermann, and Maddow. With next Tuesday's election rapidly approaching I assert the average person walking into the polling place knows nothing more about the candidates or the issues than they have seen on television.

My bold statement about stupidity comes from a personal reminder about the "real world" over the Biketoberfest weekend. Many find it surprising, but I do not have televisions; specifically I do not subscribe to cable or have an antenna to receive local stations. Curious about next week's ballot I have sought out the proposed amendments and read through the legalese and worked to understand the issues. Regarding candidates I have diligently researched with disregard to party lines, and especially worked to understand judges, commissioners, and other non-affiliated nominees. Over the last four weeks I have worked to educate you regarding labels, parties, and local politics.

I believe the last election had one of the highest voter turnouts ever among young people minorities; captivated by a polished, elegant, intellectual man from Illinois. These same people then checked other boxes on their ballots, radically changing the political landscape. A friend of mine said, "you should not be allowed to vote unless you have skin in the game." Although somewhat arrogant, the point drives home the fact that our free country allows freedom at the ballot box, even when the voter has no knowledge of the candidates or the issues.

In the final days leading to the election survey results will be reported as truth regarding how your friends and neighbors are thinking. Attack ads, and misleading advertising campaigns will be delivered at a furious pace. No matter what your party alignment and general feelings, I challenge you to find a sample ballot, study the names and prepare yourself to vote. You must take time to read the complicated proposed amendments as they will directly impact you for years to come. Remember two things: our government does not belong to Republicans and Democrats, but "We the People," and millions of Americans have died for your right to vote next week, don't waste it.

Due to Deadlines (11/3/2010)

Due to deadlines, I write this column on Saturday mornings prior to publication date and therefore it is difficult to deliver a timely column, tied directly to headlines. For instance, I wrote this five days ago, but with confidence I predicted there was a significant shift in Congress yesterday. I did not predict numbers, but predicted the headlines and commentary from the media; today you are hearing the American people "did not understand" President Obama's vision, or they were "angry" over the economy. I argue yesterday was much simpler and there is no need to overanalyze what happened.

Yesterday's outcome was about values and politicians selling out their integrity. The methods used during the health care debate showed a majority party willing to use thuggery to win an agenda. Intimidation by the Speaker, failing to hold town hall meetings and closed-door debates demonstrated Chicago-style politics used nationwide, contradictory to promises of transparency. Sadly, an examination of our local Representative Kosmas' record shows a pass given on the first vote and then a "yes" vote in round two, against the will of her constituents; a good woman sent to Washington and if she had maintained her integrity against the machine she would be returning.

With two years of legislation, failed economic policies, teleprompter speeches, extravagant travel, and excessive golf yesterday became a mandate for real "change and hope". What voters moved on was spending, an out of control congress, and failed fiscal policies. Since the last election unemployment increased, the Federal deficit increased, social security spent deficit funds, total debt increased trillions, the social agenda moved decidedly left while most Americans remain center-right, and personal freedoms were reduced.

Nearly two years ago Hillary Clinton presented Russian President Putin with a button, "Reset". Yesterday voters yesterday sent the same message to Washington and the new Republican Congress has an opportunity to echo the successes of 1994; saving America and possibly saving a President. Without the Democrat puppeteer as Speaker, Congress will find themselves free of the shackles of desperate politics and instead controlling their destiny. Congress can move quickly to save America: maintain the 2001 Bush Tax cuts, repeal healthcare, legislate spending limits as a percent of GDP, require a balanced budget, and stop the tomfoolery of passing new legislation so prevalent during the last two years. If nothing else, regardless of your political alignment, at lease the negative ads have stopped!

What Happened Last Week (11/10/2010)

Last week there was a lot more happening in America than reported. Of course everyone is aware of the change of power in the House of Representatives, and most people know Reid, Frank, Boxer, and Pelosi were re-elected. The political sage purported their own theories as to what happened, but last week was easy to explain: while the masses slept the informed went to the polls and voted. Throughout the constant barrage of political analyses there was one shift in the majority reported rarely; 19 state legislatures changed from Democrat to Republican majorities. The impact at the state level is the passage of conservative agendas, aligned with the will of the people: state influenced immigration controls, no gay marriage, gun rights will stop eroding, and we can expect more fiscal control of budgets.

In addition to the electorate changes, the twelve members of the Fed Open Market Committee, private banking individuals not elected by the people, forever changed our future. Although called "Federal Reserve" the "Fed" is as federal as "Federal Express". The group of private bankers promised to purchase $600 billion of government bonds because our debt, traditionally the stalwart of confidence to the world, has no other buyers. America will look like the 1970s, interest rates will drop further, past the already historically low rates making home and car purchases cheaper, if you can qualify for a loan or have a job, but increased prices are inevitable. By monetizing our debt, our currency was devalued and therefore it will take more dollars to buy exports. Although it sounds complicated, in the coming months the cost of everything made in China will rise, our foreign food supply will rise in cost, and OPEC will want more dollars for a barrel of crude. Gasoline should easily reach $3.40/gallon by April as OPEC is demanding a minimum $100/gallon.

What happened last week was historical, America moved politically in a direction not seen since Reconstruction (1865), recognizing the failed policies of an out of control majority. Similarly, Europe has done the same, moving Right to fight Unions, pensions for life, and nanny-state mentality. What happened last week when the Fed announced quantitative easing will also change our lives. We the People will pay today and well into the future for printing money. As we were taught in school, the Fed needs inflation to grow the economy, but inflation is really a hidden tax on us, the people.

Death and Taxes Redux (4/13/2011)

Attending funerals I reflect on death, and although inevitable we deny our mortality one statement that intrigues me is the saying, "Only two things are known; death and taxes." I know with certainty I will die and everyone around me will die, someday. Of course cause of death cannot be predicted but risks associated with death can be minimized and each of us tries to live with a goal of prolonging life and we fight death with all of our might but cannot stop its inevitability. Taxes, however, are not an absolute, but we evolved to accept taxes part of our being, just like death. Instead of continually working toward ending this other 'absolute' in our lives our society seems willing to perpetuate this self-destructive mechanism upon ourselves.

Taking a step back, maybe a better word for tax would be "privilege payment". We pay for the privilege of living in a civilized society, and this argument could be made throughout human history. Most of us are willing to contribute a nominal amount of our individual efforts to support the purported common good of the society in which we live. I accept there is a cost to civilization as I expect infrastructure for safe water, sewage disposal, defense, and transportation.

Regardless of the specifics of the individual line items that we agree to tax ourselves for, we should constantly examine the necessity. I choose to minimize the risks I take in my daily life, exercise, eat well and therefore am hopefully prolonging my life and cheating death. I argue that we no longer do the same regarding taxes and instead readily acquiesce to taxing our individual efforts and allowing the state to control and disburse them. I assert we have voluntarily enslaved ourselves to an entity that we may not be able to escape.

Death is inevitable; the process of self-destruction through taxation is not. Taxes are acceptable when presented with a true cost and benefit analysis, a clear exit strategy from the tax, and a method to provide for checks and balances against a tax. If you were taking an inventory of your personal health in an effort to ensure you were prolonging your life you would question every risk, every activity, and eliminate those that are harming you. This same analysis must be performed frequently and regularly regarding taxes. We must question every dollar that is spent and be willing to take tough measures to eliminate waste, just as you would do personally.

School Taxes (9/28/2011)

My first attempt at this week's column rubbed some folks the wrong way so I made an effort to tone down the rhetoric. I was inspired to write about senior citizens and a feeling of entitlement over a recent property tax issue. My concern is one group working to exempt themselves from a tax at the expense of those who cannot vote: school children.

With surprise, at the gym last week I saw a petition on the table for signing. The petition was to create a ballot initiative to exempt anyone aged 65 and older from the school portion of their property taxes. Sure, on the surface an argument to say, "I do not have school age children so I therefore should not pay school taxes," appears valid. However, the fallacy in the argument is it can be applied throughout the entire tax code.

Many taxes are "use" taxes: fishing license, state park fees, and even fuel taxes collected to pay for roads. Our society has agreed most other taxes are for the greater good. Researching my "refreshed" version of this column I found a Facebook page and many web sites for Seniors not paying taxes. Sadly, the consistency in the comments was one of entitlement, "I have paid enough in taxes," or my favorite, "don't we deserve a little break in our golden years." I am appalled! I see supporting schools as investments in our future. Without an educated and skilled youth our country will continue to degenerate.

The savings to her are minimal, but the impact of the entire group is substantial; millions of lost revenue per year. Personally I hate taxes and would seek to reduce any tax I pay, but I have long offered there are some necessary costs to live in a civilized society: defense, infrastructure, education, and minimal social safety nets.

Our society is changing rapidly. There are far more takers of the social security system than ever anticipated and the system cannot persist. The number of retired citizens is higher and as property owners their school property taxes are an investment in our future, and their own future. Within the next twenty years most of today's seniors will be covered in dirt, but their legacy will live as their grandchildren work to pay the debt they created.

4 CIVICS

Civics 101 – Democracy or Republic? (10/14/2009)

One of my pet peeves is lexicon misuse. This was recently reinforced by an email link I received from a friend that offered to explain our form of government and make comparisons to other common forms such as oligarchy, monarchy and anarchy. Most of us believe the United States is a democracy. However, the video I received focused on the view that our founding fathers intended the United States to be a republic. My question, of course, was what's the difference? More important, if there is a difference does it really matter?

A quick trip to the dictionary, or in this case the online version of Merriam-Webster, would most surely shed some light on the distinctions between the two words. I found a "democracy" is "government by the people; especially : rule of the majority (b) : a government in which the supreme power is vested in the people and exercised by them directly or indirectly through a system of representation usually involving periodically held free elections."

Fair enough I thought, and it sounds like the United States. So how is a republic defined? A republic is a "government having a chief of state who is not a monarch and who in modern times is usually a president (b) a government in which supreme power resides in a body of citizens entitled to vote and is exercised by elected officers and representatives responsible to them and governing according to law." Again similar to the United States in definition and at least not significantly different to help me distinguish the subtleties of the two words. Now, I felt thoroughly confused and I wondered if it mattered to the founding fathers whether our nation was to be a democracy or a republic. As a democracy our society would be subject to majority rule and the will of the people on all decisions. As a republic, it appeared that elected representation by the people would take precedence.

In today's time with Congress typically having the lowest approval ratings of all of the branches of government, couldn't we, as a democracy eliminate the House of Representatives and the Senate? With technology today this seems feasible. Anytime an issue arises we could put it to a vote of the people using the internet, our cable television remotes, or a telephone dial-in system. Arguably, the establishment of the Electoral College, our Congress, and even the inauguration dates of the President appear based on the lack of communication technology existing in 1776 as much as they do with the intent of the founding fathers. Maybe our government is more an outdated concept tied obstacles of the time.

However, a careful review of the Constitution confirms our founding fathers intended a republic. The Pledge of Allegiance, "and to the Republic for which it stands", instantly reminds us if we have any doubt. Article IV section 4 of the Constitution is quite clear, "The United States shall guarantee to every state in this Union a Republican Form of Government".

You may wonder why I am focused on the importance of what appears to be an argument in semantics. I believe our founding fathers carefully worded the Constitution to ensure its legacy would stand the test of time. Furthermore, they had personally shed blood to flee tyranny and knew that mobs and simple majority rule were not effective means of government. In a democracy, any group of individuals comprising the minority has no protection against the unlimited power of the majority. Thus, as we watch our elected representatives' debate critical issues affecting future generations, trust in our founding fathers that our republic will facilitate the best possible outcome regardless of the intensity of the debate.

Third Party Politics (3/31/2010)

My wife and I watched a movie this weekend about a recent third party presidential candidate. Although we have had third party candidates for many decades, and throughout American politics, since the 1830's the establishment of the two party system has dominated the American political process. Often the third party candidate has no more effect than "spoiler" for one of the major parties, such as Perot hurting the Republicans or Nader hurting the Democrats. Over time I would assert the public's view of third party candidates has become one of ridicule. Sadly, if citizens would take time to listen these "spoilers" typically have more wisdom and validity to their point than their mainstream opponents.

A commonality between third party candidates is their claim that the two major parties are more alike than different. Glenn Beck regularly makes these claims, pointing to both parties giving their allegiance to major corporations and political benefactors, not the American people. Ralph Nader made similar claims in his campaign as a Green Party candidate in 2000. Democrats demonize Nader as a spoiler who should have supported Al Gore and hurt the party with his insistence that Al Gore and George W. Bush were "Tweedledee and Tweedledum"--they look and act the same, so it doesn't matter which you get. Republicans similarly cried foul when Ross Perot took his campaign to the American people in his famous infomercials. Ultimately, he won 18.9% of the popular vote in 1992; the most for a third party candidate since Theodore Roosevelt in 1912, but not a single electoral vote was awarded to him.

Revolution is sewn in the seeds of discontent and it would appear those seeds are currently strewn across America as the "Tea Party" movement may be the next major opportunity for a successful third party candidate to be born into the American forefront. However, three major obstacles face this opportunity. I believe the first will be the hardest to overcome, the media. As our newspapers and televisions have suffered over the last two decades they have slowly been swallowed by a handful of major corporations that now dictate the news we see. Thus, news is no longer news, but a carefully controlled message. We know the New York Times singlehandedly contributed to the successfully election of Barak Obama by not running stories about his association with ACORN. Similarly, Ralph Nader's campaign was pushed to the back pages of the NY Times in 2000, and no mention was made on the major networks unless it was to discuss his role as spoiler. Second, the balloting rules of individual states and the Electoral College are inherently designed to prevent a third party candidate from succeeding. In America, our vote for President does not matter and is only recorded for discussion; the Electoral College elects the President. Third, the Commission on Presidential Debates will determine who participates in the debate process. Nader learned the hard way in 2000, as he could not debate the other candidates.

Ironically, one of the most admired Presidents in American history was the last third party candidate to win election; Abraham Lincoln won in 1860 on the ticket of the 8 year old Republican Party. I must wonder how many opportunities for great leaders have been missed in the last 140 years due to our system we call "democracy". As Congress and the President continue to move against the wishes of the American people I believe voters will take a stronger look at candidates that look less like the established political parties.

Liberty – Part I (7/7/2010)

I am writing this week's column on Independence Day, aka the 4th of July. I am in Washington, D.C. with my wife and children, having traveled here in our RV to show them our nation's capital and watch the fireworks from the National Mall tonight. Our first stop yesterday, was the most important highlight of the trip to me, a visit to the National Archives Museum. I wanted to share with my children the three most important documents in the world, "The Freedom Charters", or the Declaration of Independence, The Constitution, and The Bill of Rights.

Like no other nation in history, our founding fathers saw a need to create a new form of government, one free from tyranny. Men like Thomas Paine, "Common Sense", were opening the publics' eyes by creating a tool for debate to separate from a Monarchy and move to Republicanism. On July 4th, 1776 fifty-six (56) men penned their signatures to this "experiment" and risked their lives to give to future generations the "Pursuit of Life, Liberty, and Happiness." These mean, were young, idealistic, and working the land to survive and provide for their families.

Many today claim the writings and thoughts of these men are outdated and need to change with time. However, I would make another assertion; the simplicity of the singe handwritten page of the Declaration of Independence, or the four handwritten pages of the Constitution framed a government that was meant to first trust its people. As I walk around Washington, DC I now see a government that disdains its people, trusts itself, and honors itself. Our country is no longer our country, but one that belongs to a small group of elitists. This is obvious by the monuments, the size of buildings, security barriers along streets, thousands of police officers, and helicopters overflying. Ronald Reagan said, "Man is not free unless government is limited...As government expands, liberty contracts."

Since our last Independence Day our country has changed dramatically, a huge socialist move has taken place under the guise of "Change and Hope." Throughout history leaders have offered to care for their citizens, provide for them, but ultimately those experiments of evolved to dictatorships with tyrannical consequences: Mao, Hitler, Mussolini, Castro, and Stalin for example. Walking through Washington, I am proud to be an American, but like the bumper sticker on my RV says, "I love my Country…but fear my Government."

Liberty – Part II (7/14/2010)

Last week I wrote about my trip to Washington, D.C. to celebrate Independence Day with my wife and children. As I traveled through our nation's capital I saw references to freedom and liberty; celebrating our successful independence from England. Later in the week we journeyed to Williamsburg, VA and toured the Colonial Williamsburg settlement. Experiencing history again, the history I learned as a school child brought renewed appreciation to the freedom fight our forefathers faced.

I believe all men are equal in the desire for a single objective, freedom. Last year I wrote about the requirement and acceptance of taxation in trade from living in a civilized society. Similarly, our Revolutionary Heroes did not object to taxation, but to their loss of representation. In Boston the revolt began and soon the other colonies had to decide to whether to offer their support for independence. Like a child leaving home, these English subjects living in the colonies had never faced life alone and were heavily dependent on England. Facing this fear meant gaining the freedom to self-govern and envelop the spirit of the Magna Carta.

In Williamsburg, while sitting in the Courthouse I was treated to a speech and review of laws in 1770. Although subject to English law, the residents enjoyed many freedoms for which we now fight. For instance, all men were required to own a gun, and to not do so required a license for exemption. Licenses were required to do things outside the law, not those already guaranteed by the law. Today we seem to have traveled backward, requiring licenses to own guns, fish, drive a car, practice medicine, or even work as a beautician; none of which are against the law. It is this strange change, or incrementalism which silently erodes our freedom and steals our liberty.

Sadly, in my own lifetime I have seen my experience in airports change, bag searches at theme parks begin, and my newborn children required, by law, to get a social security card although he will not work for nearly two decades. "Freedom is a fragile thing and is never more than one generation away from extinction. It is not ours by inheritance; it must be fought for and defended constantly by each generation, for it comes only once to a people. Those who have known freedom and lost it, have never known it again." -- Ronald Reagan

Welcome Back (1/12/2011)

The 112th Congress began last week and last Monday night I found myself watching C-Span replaying Rep. Nancy Pelosi's inaugural speech to the 111th Congress. In January 2008 we were on the cusp of driving over an unforeseen cliff into financial Armageddon. Therefore I wonder if Ms. Pelosi's speech was sincere in its lofty promises regarding spending. She did manage to accomplish many of her goals including the passage of national health care. However, her single biggest failure was the blatant spending, supporting increases and propelling the national debt higher by $5.3 trillion dollars. One can easily argue it was not her fault, the financial crisis created a historic problem requiring spending unprecedented monies.

This past November Ms. Pelosi was re-elected by the constituents of the ultra-liberal California Bay Area 8th district identifying gay rights, social programs, and government intervention as the solution to America's problems. On the other hand, also welcomed back was Rep. John Boehner, Pelosi's outspoken critic in the House and the new House Speaker. The 112th Congress comes to Washington with great expectations to generate jobs, protect our soldiers, and provide tax relief.

Influenced by the Tea Party movement Congress started its session with a historic reading of the Constitution to remind members our founding fathers had a vision for a great republic, guided by fiscal conservatism, and relief from tyranny. I applaud the efforts to require all new bills cite the Constitutional authority given to Congress to enact it. With this citation the legislature would no longer spend many nay years awaiting the judiciary's decision to overturn unconstitutional legislation.

Sadly it appears we remain at a crossroads in American politics as even a reading of the Constitution is called pompous theater by the likes of the New York Times. Regarding the 112th's efforts, much debate will take place regarding the "Constitutionality" of their proposed actions, and only one man knows the intent of the Constitution although many consider that intent clear. I welcome back the members of Congress and hope they will look to Jefferson's writings to protect our future, "Our tenet ever was…that Congress had not unlimited powers to provide for the general welfare, …was never meant that they should provide for that welfare but by the exercise of the enumerated powers, so it could not have been meant they should raise money for purposes which the enumeration did not place under their action; consequently, that the specification of powers is a limitation of the purposes for which they may raise money." – Thomas Jefferson, 1817.

Homework (2/9/2011)

My daughter's homework recently piqued my interest while she was studying for an exam. Currently, she's taking an American Government class; learning about types of government like authoritarian, dictatorship, oligarchy, and democracy. During our studying though we came to a handout that forced me to question today's teaching as it focused on explaining the role of government. It is this question that divides left and right, Democrat and Republican. Personally I have a strong libertarian view which believes in a very limited role of government.

Reviewing her handout I learned there are seven roles taught to today's students: defense, taxation, judiciary, education, health care, transportation, and economy. I wondered how many Thomas Jefferson would include on the list and speculated three: defense, taxation, and judicial review. Seeking a more definitive answer I found only defense and judicial protection receive consensus and without taxation the rest of the list cannot exist. Sadly, I think our country has reached a crossroads in development: we can have freedom and independence to control our lives with no government involvement but risk personal loss and failure, or we can mutually combine all of our earnings and share the bounty regardless of productivity to protect our entire society against any calamity that may befall us.

I believe the second option has been tried repeatedly throughout history and most recently by the idealist Karl Marx in a quest to end class struggles; recognizing the needs of the proletariat against the bourgeoisie. Modern communism expanded on the efforts of Marx's writings with Lenin and then Stalin accelerating its spread; dictatorial regimes use communism to disguise their own human rights atrocities. Many would claim the U.S. has recently failed at the longest running experiment in capitalism and laissez faire economics allowing business to overrun the working class. However, a quick glance at American history confirms anyone, regardless of status, education, or connection can succeed to enormous wealth, unlike communist nations allow. Successes like Bill Gates, Larry Page, and Jeffrey Bezos abound and even Presidents Clinton and Obama come from the poorest of backgrounds and family struggles.

Ayn Rand concisely describes the role of government "as, the police, to protect you from criminals; the army, to protect you from foreign invaders; and the courts, to protect your property and contracts from breach or fraud by others." I believe the role of government is to allow me freedom of choice – to succeed or fail or as provided in the Declaration of Independence, "Life, Liberty, and the pursuit of Happiness.

July 4th 2011 (6/29/2011)

Last July 4th I was in Washington, D.C. with my children and wife to watch the nation's fireworks show. It was a moving experience to visit the Jefferson and Lincoln Memorials, see the Washington Monument, and more importantly to trek through the National Archives to see the Declaration of Independence and Constitution first-hand. In the last 12 months there has been a political shift in the House, political scandals, the death of Osama Bin Laden, and wars started in Libya and now Yemen. Last July 4th gas prices averaged $2.72 versus $3.70 this year, more Americans are on food stamps than ever before – 13% from last year, and housing prices have dropped more than in the Great Depression – down another 5% from last year. With bad numbers at home things must be getting better abroad, but that is far from what is occurring. The European Union appears to be entering a new crisis ignited by Greece and the Japanese earthquake is showing how desperate governments put pride before safety.

July 4th is celebration of the events of the summer of 1776 and the proclamations debated in Philadelphia in July to declare independence from the British. The two statements, "all men are created equal" and "Life, Liberty, and the pursuit of Happiness" are idolized around the world as symbolic of the freedom we have. It was September 17, 1787 that gave us the America we enjoy today; the signing of the Constitution and Bill of Rights. It did take nearly another 18 months to ratify the document, but the America I know came from the forward thinking of our early statesmen.

Many argue the Constitution should evolve with our times. In fairness I must wonder whether a document written to govern 4 million and land east of the Mississippi River where communication was measured in weeks was meant for 250 million citizens, 3000 miles shore to shore, and instantaneous access to all information available in the world. I think it is important to understand from where we came and reflect on the premise of design for a country born of hope out of fear of tyranny. Although our economy is in the toilet and more Americans than ever rely on the government dole to make ends meet, America is still a far better country than most. The visions for a strong republic and classic liberalism philosophies feel like they are fading away. As you watch fireworks this weekend, contemplate life 235 years ago and the excitement and fear in Philadelphia of starting a new country.

5 CIVIL LIBERTIES

Big Brother IS Watching (12/9/2009)

The next time you enter Wal-Mart look up and smile while walking into the store. It is stunning, but you will see a dozen cameras scanning the parking lot. Do the same at a major intersection while waiting for the light to change; note the cameras at the top of the traffic lights and count cameras watching the intersection. Willfully, the public has submitted to the pervasiveness of closed circuit television in the name of perceived safety. Ben Franklin wrote, "They who can give up essential liberty to obtain a little temporary safety, deserve neither liberty nor safety."

For years we have not been able to go in a store without "Theft TV" watching our actions in the name of crime prevention. Municipalities are adding cameras throughout their cities to prevent crimes. Currently, no one has more than the British; in 2001 the country had over one million cameras, by 2005 that number had quadrupled. One measure used is the number of cameras per thousand people. In England, the borough of Wandsworth has the highest number of CCTV cameras in London, with just fewer than four cameras per 1,000 people. Its total number of cameras - 1,113 - is more than the police departments of Boston, Johannesburg and Dublin City Council combined.

The web site, "patrolcctv.com" advertises the latest camera proposals, are vehicles equipped with CCTV. The site advertizes it "stabilizes images, reads license plates at 250FT." These always on systems analyze license plate numbers to search for a relationship between vehicles, names, and criminals. Furthermore, the date, time, and GPS location of the vehicle may be stored for future reference in a database. Just like software scanning state databases of driver's license photos for "probable hits" the same will be done for vehicles. Ultimately, all of us now stand in a police line-up every day by virtue of having a driver's license and are under constant stake-out by driving vehicles.

The saturation of cameras in Britain and the United States has soared due to successes when major crimes are caught on film. Of course, the camera makes police work much easier and the public tends to feel a sense of safety. I on the other hand am bothered by the pervasiveness of CCTV and the potential for misuse by authorities or private agencies. I believe government, when given the opportunity, will ultimately use data-mining, facial recognition software, and other surveillance means to identify potential criminals. At the same time, I believe such use suffers from a high probability of potential error. Sadly, the burden of proof will shift from one of guilt made by prosecutors to one of innocence argued by citizens.

On one side the claim for cameras is obvious: increased public safety and crime prevention. On the other hand, there appears to be no conclusive evidence cameras are a crime deterrent. We believe George Orwell's "1984" would never happen, but we are now living with Big Brother watching everything we do. Willfully, we submitted in the belief of safety and instead, like Franklin warned, have lost our liberties. Look up and smile the next time you think you are alone.

Civil Rights (12/16/2009)

Civil rights are a class of rights and freedoms protecting individuals from unwarranted government action and ensuring one's ability to participate in the civil and political life of the state without discrimination or repression. I believe most of us take these rights for granted and have no appreciation for these freedoms conveyed upon us. Furthermore, we turn a blind eye to the litigation by brave citizens taking place everyday across the country, as there generally is no publicity, but yet these court cases effect all of us in ways we cannot imagine.

Protection of civil rights is not an issue of political values, whether you are on the Right or the Left. These are rights neutral to politics, but often the court cases surrounding an issue become the source of political argument instead of the issue at hand. For example, my wife and I recently watched the movie, "The People vs. Larry Flynt" covering the landmark Supreme Court Case about first amendment rights and protection of speech. When the arguments were made the Moral Majority dominated public opinion and the Right was blind to the larger concern of speech versus Larry Flynt's association with the porn industry. Ironically, this case provides Rush Limbaugh and Glenn Beck with the freedom they need to criticize and satirize the current president.

In Georgia a current case is before the Federal Court of Appeals regarding gun rights and carrying guns on MARTA (the public transit system) when properly licensed with a firearm's permit. Anti-gun groups from the Left argue these rights should not persist in the name of safety or terrorist concerns. From a civil rights standpoint though, the interesting fact in this case is the 4th Amendment protection from unreasonable search and seizure. The Georgia Carry Organization (GCO) has argues stopping a citizen, who is committing no crime, to check ID and firearms licensure is the same as the Supreme Court's previously affirmed position that police cannot stop a motorist, who is committing no crime, just to check for a valid driver's license. A loss in a case like this will permit law enforcement to stop anyone regardless of circumstances.

Similar to the case above, every American has willfully given up civil rights since the terrorist acts of September 11th, 2001. To cross the borders between states every traveler is subject to verification of identity and search including scanning, pat-down, and removal of shoes. Of course, this takes place at airports and applies to millions of daily passengers. With no clear directive, TSA has taken wide sweeping liberties to extend authority to include screening for crimes which may or may not be in progress. For instance, in 2008 an aide, Steve Bierfeldt, to Congressman Ron Paul was detained by TSA at St. Louis-Lambert International Airport and questioned although no crime was committed. In this case, he refused to answer questions regarding why he was carrying $4,700 in cash and had no reason to comply because no crime was in process and it was a violation of his 4th Amendment rights. Fortunately for all travelers, he prevailed and TSA is slowly issuing new policies limiting screenings to searches for "terrorist related" items.

It is easy to criticize Larry Flynt if you are offended by pornography. It is easy to criticize the actions of the GCO if you do not support gun rights. It is easy to defend the actions of TSA in the name of protection. However, it is hard to stand up to the government, fight battles in court, and protect civil rights. These are the unsung heroes of the Left and the Right, fighting battles for all of us each day.

Protected Speech (12/30/2009)

I sit in the middle on this page with an objective to raise points of interest to anyone, regardless of political view. Writing on this page brings scrutiny to my opinions and exposes myself to debate and argument. I have learned it takes courage to stand in front of the crowd for what I believe, and I always work to ensure there are no personal attacks in my writing, but often I see columnists and bloggers using personal attacks in an effort to drive home their point. Fueling these attacks is the veil of anonymity; no longer signing a letter or a blog response with your name and address creating an inflammatory environment. Furthermore, I do not believe the First Amendment was intended to protect anonymous speech, but the Supreme Court has taken a different view.

I absolutely believe our democracy thrives on protected speech; it differentiates us from the oppression found around the world when ideas and opinions are given. Appropriately, libel and slander laws are also in place to prevent abuse of protected speech.

A few recent examples of my concern over whether anonymous speech is protected are important as I feel the cowardice of anonymity fuels defamatory personal attacks. For example, Tiger Woods is fighting in the Court of public opinion. Legitimate writers are identifiable and must "source" their comments. Sadly though, I have read news articles on various web sites where anonymous bloggers attack Tiger's character and make crude comments about him personally. These anonymous people don't know him and have no basis for those comments, but behind the veil of anonymity these people weakly assert defamatory opinions.

Similarly, people either love or hate Sarah Palin. As a country we are as divided on feelings about her as we are on college football in Florida. We all know the story of Palin and her rise to the highest position of leadership in Alaska, but yet people attack her personally. Opinions focus not on Palin's accomplishments as a politician, but instead follow David Letterman's method of crude, personal attacks. A quick look at the Huffington Post article regarding the Newsweek cover featuring Palin's "legs" showed over 1,000 commentators and I must wonder how the tone of those comments would change had real names and addresses been used.

Personally, I feel the problem with the protection of anonymous speech is it allows for cowardice and unfounded statements. But, the Supreme Court has repeatedly ruled anonymous speech is protected. The much cited 1995 Supreme

Court ruling in McIntyre vs. Ohio Elections Commission reads: "Protections for anonymous speech are vital to democratic discourse. Allowing dissenters to shield their identities frees them to express critical, minority views . . . Anonymity is a shield from the tyranny of the majority. . . . It thus exemplifies the purpose behind the Bill of Rights, and of the First Amendment in particular: to protect unpopular individuals from retaliation . . . at the hand of an intolerant society."

Although protected, sadly anonymous speech typically leaves the door open to defamation and the burden to prove otherwise is on the victim. Thus, this empowers questionable publications and writings and can sway public opinion on unfounded claims. I will continue to sign my name and always write with the understanding that I stand by my opinions and am not ashamed to hide behind anonymity. I encourage you to consider what you want to say and whether it is anonymity or your beliefs that give you the strength to share your opinion.

Incremental Destruction (3/10/2010)

Never underestimate the power of incrementalism or "shock" negotiation, effective methods to promote an agenda, even when fully opposed. Generally this seems too far-fetched for people to believe because they fall victim to the idea certain changes could never take place in America. For years I have asserted this is an effective method for change and destructive to our lifestyle and freedoms. Currently we are confronted with a plethora of assaults on our liberties, and when faced with a full assault, gaining any concessions makes it feel like a battle has been won, although loss occurred.

Examples of this incremental assault are obvious, our banks and automakers have been nationalized. You may be tempted to cry foul on this assertion, but we know the stories over the past year with the CEO of General Motors having been fired by the POTUS and the American taxpayer becoming the largest stockholder of GM. We have watched votes in Congress pushed through under cover of night, in contradiction to the President's claim to make bills available online for five days before signing. Last week Democrats reiterated plans to move forward with healthcare, regardless of support from the minority party, or the people. The latest Rasmussen Poll, March 1, 2010, shows "52% of U.S. voters continue to oppose the plan proposed by the president and congressional Democrats." When President Obama won the election by 53% of the popular vote he claimed he had a "clear mandate" from the people. By the same thought process, I would claim Congress and the President have a "clear mandate" from the people to stop healthcare.

In the early 1980's proposals for a national identity system were proposed. Quickly this idea was squashed by public opinion and concerns over "1984" becoming the norm. Something else happened though and a national identity system slowly materialized. Today, you can not apply for insurance, attend college, get a loan, apply for a credit card, or apply for a gun license without providing a social security number. Incrementally, a national identity system successfully came into our lives. It took about fifteen years to become normal, with citizens willfully providing this information, "many medical providers are using the SSN as a patient identifier, thus hardening the number as a de facto national identifier," testified by David Miller before the National Committee on Vital Health Statistics in a hearing in Chicago, Jul. 21, 1998.

I have previously discussed the intrusion of video cameras into all aspects of our lives. I personally noted this during the last week: at an intersection where I counted six cameras atop traffic lights, and a Wal-Mart where 17 separate cameras monitored the parking lot. Reiterating this concern further was a March 3, 2010 USA Today article, "Police partner with license plate readers." In this article many municipalities are identified with the technology promoting claims to stop stolen vehicles and monitor crimes. Arguably, these governments have an opportunity to first increase revenue in these dire economic times, but more importantly they may track and save vehicle movements for potential misuse at a later date.

Over many objections our government continues to defy the wants of its citizens. Incrementally, through legislation, systems abuses of social security, monitoring citizens with cameras, and using the courts to re-interpret legislation and constitutionality, my children will never know what freedom is. Their lives will be changed by constant monitoring, national identity, and nanny-state mandates more akin to movies like "1984" and "Brazil". Incrementally, tyranny is becoming the new normal, but yet we feel relief to have any freedom left.

More from Big Brother (4/21/2010)

On April 8th an article appeared in USA Today about a court case involving the release of aircraft tail numbers through a Freedom of Information Act filing. In summary, the FAA tracks tail numbers of aircraft flight plans, this data is fed to a computer system and is available on public web sites like FlightAware.com. The FAA stores this information for a period of 90 days and ultimately purges it from their systems. Commercial, corporate and private flights are all tracked. As web sites and internet usage became more prevalent over the last 15 years, so did concerns over privacy; prompting the National Business Aircraft Association (NBAA) to work with the FAA to provide a mechanism to block tail numbers from public view. Without reason, a person or company could request this protection. Why, you might wonder? Prior to the protection, the most obvious examinations of the data were businesses spying on competitors, and stalking of high-profile individuals.

My concern in this court case is the misuse of information and the right to privacy. The successful argument to obtain data was made under the argument the air traffic control system is public and therefore no justification exists for a public entity to protect, or block the elements of this data. With the current populist movement taking place in America though one must wonder how many liberties citizens are willing to give up in the name of public information. It is easy to argue this data should be public when promoting anger at rich executives over the use of their expensive aircraft. However, the stockholders elect the Board of Directors who protects the use of assets within a company, and therefore makes companies more profitable, funding pension plans and retirement for millions. For whatever purpose: stalking, tracking competition, or as a hobby though one must wonder where the line is between privacy and public interest.

Similar to tail number tracking, several months ago I wrote about municipalities purchasing camera systems to scan and collect license plate information. In this case the municipalities argue the data will be purged within 30-60 days and the purpose of collection is for the public interest of tracking criminal activity. In my opinion it is easy to leap to the same conclusion as the FAA data, information collected by a public entity, for whatever purpose and regardless of whether it is purged, shall be made public. In our capitalistic society it won't take long for a savvy web programmer to build a database, real-time feed, and search engine to make license plate data available. Like Flightaware, linking this to the owner of record, again a public DOT database, and make, model, and color of car will be effortless. Of course, with a date and time stamp of location from traffic cameras, using these data collection sites to know a person's whereabouts at any time will be effortless. Thus, an employer can monitor whether a work from home employee is out and about during the day, or a divorce case could use such data to focus on the whereabouts of a spouse, or the paparazzi would know where an individual frequents.

I have previously quoted Ben Franklin regarding trading liberty for safety and my concerns remain the same. I see a trend, one where we willingly allow ourselves to be tracked, whether for credit bureaus, healthcare databases, aircraft travel or driving a car. We are now a society under constant monitoring and surveillance, and we willingly participated. In this case it is not law enforcement, but angry, jealous citizens watching each other.

George Bush's Worst Decision (4/28/2010)

During the eight years of the George W. Bush presidency America changed significantly. Conservatives claim economic policies worked, but many were inherited from Bill Clinton. They claim the representation of smaller government fueled the economic boom of the aughts, but the truth is the largest expansion of government services and spending took place, until President Obama exponentially eclipsed those figures, and America's civil liberties were willfully eroded. Repeatedly I have written about exchanging our liberties for the perception of safety, but no president did more to change our view of the world than "W" in the months and years following September 11th, 2001.

Congress immediately started working on the Patriot Act after the September 11th attacks. Even government marketing proponents make it hard to argue because it would make one "unpatriotic" to disagree. Among the worst elements of the Patriot Act that stole liberties was Title II, covering surveillance procedures. Although one could hope the original intent was to provide additional surveillance on enemies of the United States, the enhancements contained within this statute expanded the scope and availability of wiretapping and surveillance orders. Subpoenas delivered to internet service providers were expanded to include not only "the name, address, local and long distance telephone toll billing records, telephone number or other subscriber number or identity, and length of service of a subscriber" but also session times and durations, types of services used, communication device address information, payment method and bank account and credit card numbers.

Several other sections of the Patriot Act, Title III, anti-money-laundering to prevent terrorism, and Title IV, border security, have changed our daily lives. When dealing with any financial institution we must provide proof of American citizenship to open an account. Cash transactions in excess of $10,000 must be reported, and all brokers and bankers are trained to spy on you – ordered to report any odd patterns in financial transactions. Border security has limited our ability to take a weekend jaunt to the Bahamas, requiring a passport to return to our own country.

Finally, the most notorious provision in the Patriot Act is Title VIII, the Terrorism Criminal Law and it redefined the term "domestic terrorism" to broadly include mass destruction as well as assassination or kidnapping as a terrorist activity. The definition includes activities intended to "intimidate or coerce a civilian population," "influence the policy of a government by intimidation or coercion," or are undertaken "to affect the conduct of a government by mass destruction, assassination, or kidnapping" while in the jurisdiction of the United States. On one hand, under the guise of the attacks of September 11th, the provision arguably makes sense to allow prosecution of the foreign terrorists. However, a dramatic shift has recently taken place by the current party in power to invoke the elements of this section and call into question the activities of Americans peacefully protesting and asserting their First Amendment rights to free speech. Both Homeland Security Secretary Janet Napolitano and former President Bill Clinton have referred to citizens engaging in tax protests, arguing against health care, or disagreeing with the current administration as domestic terrorists.

Our government is asserting power it was never intended to have and I believe the Founding Fathers would be appalled at the efforts currently underway. It appears George Bush's legacy is shrouded in reigning in the citizens of the United States, to control them and create an environment focused on monitoring and surveillance. The First Amendment is no longer about freedom of speech, to willfully speak, but containment of speech within the bounds of the Patriot Act.

Police State (7/28/2010)

Last week I came across a news article that left me feeling uneasy. For perspective, I read various news sites every day, everything from the New York Times, Washington Times, and even the Times UK. I look to CNN, Pravda, Huffington Post and Breitbart for a variety and balance of news. As you know, I have previously written about CCTV (Closed Circuit Television) and the invasion of cameras creating questionable civil rights questions. Additionally, we have seen the expansion of citizens using cameras to capture incredible moments on tape: plane crashes, auto accidents, tornadoes, and questionable arrests and police brutality. It is the last category that concerns me.

About six months ago I noticed a trend in some of the news articles I was reading: police were arresting those who videotape them! I came across these articles on fringe, strong civil liberties web sites commenting on states that were using outdated wiretap laws to prevent citizens from videotaping an arrest. Under this premise, the states require both parties to give consent. Of course, law enforcement was not consenting and instead threatening arrest if videotaping continued. Last week I saw a similar article, but this time it was carried by ABC news, "Growing Number of Prosecutions for Videotaping the Police", by Ray Sanchez (07/19/2010). The article describes cases in New Hampshire, Maryland, and Florida where wiretapping laws are used to arrest citizens as I described.

I believe law enforcement officers are employees of the public; ultimately they work for us. In countries like China, North Korea, the former USSR, and former East Germany the police worked for the government and were charged with watching citizens. In these countries law enforcement runs rampant with brutality, torture, and intimidation. I argue, like Florida's governing laws, that operating in the sunshine eliminates these horrors. Like our right to bear arms, or speak freely, our rights to hold public government and law enforcement officers accountable is paramount to our personal safety.

What would have happened to Rodney King had news helicopters not caught his beating? As hard as I try, I cannot come up with a valid argument to justify preventing a citizen from videotaping his own arrest. When a law enforcement officer dons his uniform he is a servant of the public, not a Gestapo officer given free rein to operate in darkness with no one looking.

Obama is Right (9/8/2010)

This is probably the most concerning column I have written, not because I agree with the President but because the issue is sensitive, to both sides. Currently, whether to build Park51 (a.k.a. Ground Zero Mosque) is driving passionate public debates. Hesitantly, President Obama voiced his opinion two weeks ago when he said the right to build the project was constitutionally protected. The following day he made further comments stating while constitutionally protected, it may be in bad taste. I must agree with both of his comments. While it may be in bad taste, I do not believe it is a community center designed to protect, or possibly sympathize to Islamic terrorists as has been asserted by some in the media. Ultimately, the court of public opinion will either empower the developers and those funding the project, or send them packing.

I am disturbed by talk radio pundits flummoxing methods. Other than to inflame an ill-informed public there is no other purpose for the front-page debate. The fallacy of the current argument comes from the presumption if terrorists are Muslim then all Muslims are terrorists. I take issue because living in the south, as a white male; I am stereotyped as a racist redneck by the argument racist rednecks are southern white males. Similarly, a German born in the 1920's is not automatically a Nazi. What has been lost in the argument propelled center stage is the right to build a place of worship, as protected by the First Amendment of the Constitution. The same people who herald the constitution in arguments against healthcare, bailouts, and social programs are quick to stomp the same document when it does not meet their needs.

There are many aspects of the Constitution which may not conveniently fit our desires and likes. However, if we remain consistent in our application, trusting the truths set forth by the founding fathers we will not go wrong. In the case of Park51, it is clear there is no constitutional violation to build. The decision to build is purely local and is governed by the zoning laws, planning commissions, and local electorate. Does it feel good to support building the project? No, but the more important issue at hand is support of the Constitution in the face of our enemies, asserting what separates our country from those who attack us in the name of God.

We Need to Burn Qurans (9/10/2010)

I am disappointed this afternoon, Thursday the 9th of September, after reading reports that Pastor Terry Jones has announced his church will not burn the Quran on Saturday, September 11th, the ninth anniversary of the day America was attacked by Muslim extremists. Last week I wrote in support of the project in New York, building a mosque at Ground Zero. Constitutionally the right to build the Mosque is guaranteed; however distasteful. Similarly, Pastor Jones' right to burn the Quran is guaranteed; again, however distasteful. I would hope our military could defend itself, but that appears questionable based on public comments.

What truly concerns me is the world's willingness to cow tow to the Muslim extremists and threats. Are we to believe the world's largest superpower, the USA, and our western allies cannot defend citizens against threats from religious zealots who have become a political movement set on killing all who disagree with them? President Kennedy's Secretary of State, Dean Rusk, said "appeasing the aggressor only makes him more aggressive." Repeatedly, this political movement, called Islam, has attacked innocent civilians worldwide: December 1992 in Yemen, 1993

WTC in New York, 1998 Kenya and Tanzania US Embassies killing 200 and injuring 5000, October 2000 USS Cole, 2000 Rizal Day Bombings in the Philippines, WTC 9/11/2001, 2007 Algiers Bombing, 2008 Danish Embassy, and the 2009 Little Rock Arkansas Recruitment building. Additionally, although not tied directly to Al-Qaeda, the Ft. Hood Massacre, failed 2009 Northwest Airlines bombing, and the failed Times Square bombing were also in "the name of Allah."

Our President offers apologies to the nations of the world that oppress their mothers, daughters, and wives. The same nations with state established religion, censorship, and political oppression. He finds reasons to coddle our enemies, fails to retaliate, and explains we will withdraw troops to satisfy the demands of the petroleum-based kingdoms harboring the Jihadists who hate us. Our enemy issues "fatwa" for denigrating their political idols and writings, Muhammad, Allah and the Quran. Just check with Solomon Rushdie and the creators of South Park. Pastor Jones is considered by many a red-neck racist extremist; maybe he is a guy with the cojones to stand up to our enemy. Most saddening is General Patreaus' concern for troop safety which makes me wonder who is winning the war. It appears 2,983 died on 9/11/2001 in vain and there can only be one conclusion: we must all live in fear of Islam.

Ants and Grasshoppers (11/24/2010)

I dictated this column ten days ago when the TSA backlash was first starting. Since 9/11 I have been questioning the policies of George Bush and the creation of the Department of Homeland Security. In October 2002 I had a letter published in the News-Journal predicting new airport security measures were similar to Nazi Germany and the Soviet Union. Removing shoes came next, I tried to resist but after being placed on the "TSA Watch List" and threatened by TSA I ultimately acquiesced and felt alone trying to stop this intrusion. TSA demonstrated its stupidity with its policy on liquids, watching me drink a bottle of

Dasani water, clear and pure; requiring its disposal because it will explode.

Several weeks ago I saw a Tampa television station dutifully reporting about a multi-jurisdictional task force at the Greyhound bus station where FHP, TSA, and Border police were checking papers and searching passengers. The week before an Atlanta television station likewise reported about a comparable task force stopping trucks inbound on I-20 to pass through full size X-ray machines, check papers, and be searched. Sadly, Americans willfully reported they were glad to experience the inconvenience and felt safer, and no one seemed to question the right of the government or the warrantless search performed in direct contradiction to the Constitution, "The right of the people to be secure in their persons, houses, papers, and effects, against unreasonable searches and seizures, shall not be violated, and no Warrants shall issue, but upon probable cause, supported by Oath or affirmation, and particularly describing the place to be searched, and the persons or things to be seized."

This issue has moved beyond the requirement for airline security. Bush's moves after 9/11, in the name of fighting terrorism, stole freedoms from Americans, undoing over 225 years of liberty: the Patriot Act created unprecedented warrantless spying, Homeland Security employees over 200,000 with a budget of $52 billion, and the relatively unknown support of the Courts to establish "Constitution Free Zones". While you watch your elderly mother, wife, or teenage daughter undergo an intrusive, pat-down search, ask yourself by what authority has the government asserted this right.

The current fight is about the Ant and the Grasshopper, and the general failure of Americans to understand their Constitutional rights. We, the ants, are trying to resist the government grasshopper. If we succeed, we undo years of authoritarian success by the grasshopper.

It's Easy they just submit
TSA
XRAY
Ashes
Nelson 12/25

My TSA Cartoon (12/25/2010)

I was incredibly concerned and appalled with the actions TSA took in late 2010. Sadly their efforts have been effective and Americans refuse to resist the oppression upon them. It was out of this frustration on Christmas Day when I was motivated to draw a cartoon satirically examining the actions of TSA. There is no reason for the scanners used at airports, and there is absolutely no reason to use them at ball games, bus stations, or high school proms. However, we continue to allow their use and willfully submit to the government's disregard for the 4th Amendment.

Family Conversations (12/1/2010)

Like many families this past weekend more relatives than I can count on fingers and toes gathered for dinner. In addition to Thanksgiving, we gathered for birthdays for my son's third and my wife's birthday. Instantly apparent with families is the irony of different political opinions and world views, but yet having close relations. Of course, with the news of the weekend we found ourselves discussing shopping, football, and inevitably TSA's new airport search procedures.

I was surprised, and left feeling hopeful, because we did not have our normal disagreements; there was consensus over TSA going too far to search passengers. For proper perspective it is important to understand my extended family lives in New York and was all heavily impacted by the deaths of 3,000 Americans nine years ago. There is no dissent among us that security is required and we are aligned that the current methods are clearly out of hand and nonsensical. If asked, we decided we should be allowed to set policy for TSA; making travel better for all Americans. Our suggestions are as follows:

- Don't be stupid. Enough said.

- If a passenger is drinking water, allow him to take water through security as we are certain water is not explosive.
- No one should be subjected to backscatter x-rays, radiation is bad and the TSA workers should be provided radiation badges and OSHA protection.
- Profiling is a must, not racial or religious, but behavior profiling. The Israelis question passengers and look for nervousness. We can do the same.
- If a frequent flyer buys a round trip ticket, allow him to pass through security, saving time for him and allowing TSA to focus on true threats.
- We feel all children under 12 and grandmothers over 60 can be eliminated as possible terror threats.

Reading the news of the attempted Christmas tree bombing in Oregon this weekend further demonstrates that no amount of security checkpoints is going to stop terror in our country. It appears an excellent sting operation was carried out by the FBI, leading to an arrest. Scarily, it confirmed once again the sickness of this religious enemy whose only satisfaction will come when all people who disagree with them are wiped from the earth. After this weekend I am confident most Americans want safety, but without stupidity and the loss of civil rights. I am not the enemy; please don't treat me like one.

Wikisuccess (12/8/2010)

I have been stunned by the number of times I have asked friends and family about Wikileaks and their opinion last week and they knew nothing. Although Wikileaks was splashed all over the headlines, sadly it appears Cybermonday is far more important to most Americans. Last week the talk show personalities and government officials were quick to offer their condemnations, calling the actions of Wikileaks treasonous and criminal. Anytime the media, government, and the entire political spectrum agree it is worth considering the contrarian position.

Personally, I have a strong contradictory opinion in support of Wikileaks and want to make a case for my opinion.

I have watched Wikileaks evolve over the last several years as a safe haven for whistleblower journalism. Julian Assange is an Australian born hacker who ran a software company and is the public persona of Wikileaks. The catalyst for the web site was capturing internet traffic in China, observations and secret emails by the Chinese government several years ago shared by dissidents who required extreme protection for fear of ultimate retaliation by the Chinese. With the protections of Swedish law regarding anonymity to sources of the Press, secure servers around the world, and safe drop boxes for information Wikileaks became the ultimate whistleblower web site. Not only has the site shared government secrets, but individuals have posted corporate details leading to arrests.

In April 2010, after funding and server problems, Assange splashed Wikileaks across the front pages of the news worldwide with the release of secret documents describing U.S. killings of civilians in Iraq in 2007. In July 2010 Wikileaks released the "Afghan War Diaries" and Assange was instantly condemned by both the press and government for recklessly putting troops in harm's way through the document release. However, the Afghanistan documents brought to light government cover-ups regarding friendly fire and civilian casualties. At the time, I researched this release wondering about the legality and learned of a similar, earth shattering release of government information made by Daniel Ellsberg in 1971, "The Pentagon Papers." Ellsberg was vindicated by the Supreme Court ruling the Constitution guarantees anonymity, at least in the area of political discourse.

With the release of last week's documents, now labeled "cablegate", Assange has become a permanent thorn to the U.S. government. Both sides of the aisle have called his acts treasonous and are seeking his arrest. He is reviled by many and wanted by Interpol, for consensual sex without a condom in Sweden. I argue the headlines are made to discredit Assange and tarnish his public reputation. Sarah Palin has blasted Assange,

Clinton accused him of an 'attack' on the world, and Senator Lieberman successfully shutdown servers and related Wikileaks documents in the United States.

The documents show embarrassing corruption in the Afghanistan war, orders to spy on delegates to the United Nations by Secretary Clinton, and accusations of mafia like activities by the Russian government. I believe the documents show the true nature of our government, and governments worldwide, an elitist class of buffoons in charge of public policy using their positions of power to promote personal self interests. We all learn in high school we should live our lives as if our actions are to make front page headlines on the New York Times. In this case, with the release of documents dating back 40 years the true opinions and ineptness of our government officials is now public.

Those against the release of Wikileaks argue the documents will result in the loss of life to secretly placed operatives and erode progress of political negotiations, but no one has died as a result of Wikileaks. Cablegate has shed light on African governments stealing billions for personal gain, negotiations by the U.S. with terrorist nations, and acknowledgment of civilian loss of life in our wars. I am shocked the media is not more supportive of Wikileaks and can only assume the embarrassment of being "scooped" by one outside their ranks, similar to Matt Drudge during the Clinton years, has alienated support.

I argue government must be held to the highest standard, one that operates with ultimate transparency. Without the spotlight of transparency the citizens are subject to corruption, theft of public funds in the treasury, disregard of the law, and in some cases death. Assange promises the next release will reveal details of a large bank institution's handling of the financial crisis. I believe public opinion and the media anchors will offer applause when Wikileaks offers the same insights inside a private corporation and comments similar to those made by our government leaders inside a board room would make the late night talk show monologues rife with jokes, not condemnation. I want my government held accountable and operating with the highest integrity and moral fortitude, I applaud Assange and his courageousness. History will reflect his actions as critical to the safety of citizens worldwide and changing the way government operates.

As I write this column, Saturday December 4th, 2010, the Wikileaks.org web site I visited multiple times earlier in the week is no longer accessible. Internet purists are working on new technologies to bypass government interventions and maintain ultimate freedom of information on the web. I do not live in China, I do not want censorship, and I do not want the tyranny of a government hiding from its own illegal acts.

Free Speech (12/15/2010)

I argue the most important freedom we have under the Constitution is the right to Freedom of Speech. It is interpreted as the right to speak freely without censorship or limitation. As defined in our own First Amendment to the Constitution, "*Congress shall make no law respecting an establishment of religion, or prohibiting the free exercise thereof; or abridging the freedom of speech, or of the press; or the right of the people peaceably to assemble, and to petition the Government for a redress of grievances.*"

Sadly though, something happened over the last century, accelerating rapidly over the last two decades. I previously wrote freedom of speech must remain free of tests, and the most important speech is one making us uncomfortable, but yet allowed. It is free speech protecting news media, web sites, and our access to information. We take for granted the freedom of the Internet and our assumed rights to read, review, and see any content. Of course, we are aware countries like China and North Korea censor their citizens' access to web sites and news, especially political discourse contradicting their governments. We assume this will not happen in America, but quite the opposite is true.

Last week Senator Lieberman proudly announced his success pressuring Amazon.com to remove Wikileaks from its servers.

Bill O'Reilly called for the execution of Wikileaks' Julian Assange on his television show and Sarah Palin similarly did the same. The narrow-mindedness of these pundits is more concerning than the actions of Assange. Our willingness to have "hate speech" protections in America caused a young man in Kentucky to find himself sentenced to prison for three years last week after writing a poem titled, "The Sniper," a concerning poem narrating the assassination of President Obama, but one that should be protected by the First Amendment nonetheless.

Many would argue some speech is bad, but I assert you must accept all speech to truly enjoy freedom of speech. The writings of Thomas Paine and Thomas Jefferson granted our liberties and released us from tyranny. Using today's standards their writings are treasonous and require "balance" and an investigation by Homeland Security would ensue with both men finding themselves on Domestic Terrorist watch lists; there would be no American Revolution. No matter how uncomfortable, the right to criticize and question our government leaders gave us our freedoms and we must continue to monitor and fight to keep this right to free speech. "*Censorship reflects society's lack of confidence in itself. It is a hallmark of an authoritarian regime*," Potter Stewart.

Welcome 2011 (aka 1984) (12/29/2010)

Orwell's 1984 is an unbelievable tale imagined in 1949 focusing on government surveillance and mind control. Since 9/11 Americans have followed the Orwellian path: trading liberty for the perception of safety. Like Sheep, there is no resistance stepping into body scanners, allowing our mothers, daughters, and wives submission to hands of questionable authority, and acceptance of cameras and data mining to predict actions. Our same ruling elite, like the "Inner Party" exempts itself from the rules and regulations put upon "We the People".

My goal is not to pontificate doom and gloom, but raise awareness and challenge the status quo. I must wonder why a NFL football dominates television ratings when our society is collapsing around us. Much of the change thrust upon us was incrementally small and came slowly after 9/11. However, I believe there has been an acceleration of lost liberties in the last two years. For example: a pilot challenging TSA's procedures last week had his home raided by Federal Authorities under administrative rules creating a warrantless search; TSA announced further silly rules scrutinizing Thermos bottles; passengers cannot take water through security as it may explode; *Wired* magazine detailed government collection and scrutiny of credit card and store loyalty card data; *Google* through *StreetView* and other data mining practices announced predictive behavioral searches; municipalities are investing in license plate readers to track all traffic in their communities; you cannot enter a store or public place without CCTV recording and forever storing your image; without warrants the NSA is listening to phone and email traffic; purchase of certain over-the-counter drugs requires logging your identity in a government database although no law is broken; Attorney General Eric Holder shared in an interview with Diane Sawyer last week American citizens require surveillance to stop homegrown terror; passage of Net Neutrality was the first step toward an ID requirement to access the web; and Janet Napolitano announced Wal-mart will install televisions nationwide to broadcast the "If you See Something, Say Something" campaign encouraging us to report on others.

I do not have confidence in the government, nor do I trust the government to maintain its integrity. By the government's admission we need to question those who exercise First Amendment Rights, have certain political bumper stickers, belong to organizations like the NRA, and criticize the United Nations. As 2011 comes upon us I challenge you to watch the weekly announcements of new government "security" programs and ask, "Why?" *Big Brother is watching you.* – George Orwell.

Cairo – Do Americans Riot (01/30/2011)

Several weeks ago uprisings in Tunisia dominated the evening news and daily papers. Most Americans are quick to dismiss such events, and why not? Steven Tyler's performance on "*American Idol*" or the choosing of 20-something millionaires to play in the Super Bowl delude the masses; appearing far more important than citizens risking their lives for freedom. I too have felt the challenge to understand, but in college I watched Chinese students challenge communist regime and ultimately give their lives in Tiananmen Square to demonstrate the human rights violations of their government. Growing up I knew the communists of the U.S.S.R. regularly violated individual freedoms and imprisoned citizens behind the iron curtain. Through Hollywood movies I learned more about the fight after World War II and my history classes tried to explain the actions of authoritarianism and dictatorships.

Although many arguments about the cause may be made, the issues in Cairo this week are driven by 30 years of authoritarian rule under President Hosni Mubarak and a discontent youth rebelling against his authority. But the recent riots are not new, and by no means ultimately represent the underlying problems in a country desirous of democracy but operating with an ancient mentality. On November 24, 2010 a Christian was killed, 100 arrested and 3,000 demonstrators protested the razing of a new Christian church built without a permit. Under Ottoman law a permit is required to build a Christian church, in contrast Mosques are built easily and regularly without review of a state authority. Today many assertions are being made in the media that the riots are religious in nature, but local reporting and blogging, held an opposite view. Instead, the riots are the result of 30 years of oppression and dictatorship and inspired by the Jasmine Revolution in Tunisia.

As the World's policeman the American citizenry believes our own government is above such actions and the riots we watch overseas could not occur here. My wife and I had a conversation this week about Americans and whether riots would take place here. Coincidentally I am reading a book, *The Emerging Police State* by William Kunstler and together we watched *Battle in Seattle*, chronicling protests against the World Trade Organization. Skeptically I listen to the outrageous conspiracy claims of Alex Jones and wonder if any truth inspires. As I learn more though I have discovered striking parallels between the radical claims of the left and the right; the common thread leading to a questioning of our government's actions. Uprisings have occurred on our soil, and many are similar to Egypt: spurred by youth and ideological believers desperate for change and an opportunity to be heard. Sadly, like Egypt, death has come upon those who question the United States government or the corporations profiting and seeking protections through the rule of law.

Kunstler's book is a compilation of speeches made through the years and inspired by his battles for justice. In my opinion it is easy to condemn the actions of those we do not like, but it is more important to defend the application of justice when we like it least. From a speech in 1971, with memories of Kent State fresh, long forgotten to the annals of time and unknown to anyone under age 40 today, he indicts the government for condoning the slaughter of unarmed students, using the law to fabricate evidence and justify its actions. In the most disgusting example, the Grand Jury which is supposed to provide protection from the law, but serves as an agency of the government, found the National Guard justified in shooting, although no student sniper existed and it was a Major's discharge of his sidearm that prompted spraying the crowd with bullets. Furthermore, the Grand Jury recommended .22-caliber bullets should be used against future student demonstrators instead of the larger, more harmful caliber M-1.

Forty years later, in the summer of 2010, Pittsburg was shut down and noise suppression cannons were used to hold off G-20 demonstrators. No one was killed, but our government has mechanisms to slow and prevent demonstrations. Likewise, the movie "*Battle in Seattle*" shows the offensive measures police and National Guard took against WTO protesters in 1999. Since then "Exclusion Zones" have been created and are defined as "areas where protesters are legally prohibited." A quick read of the Bill of Rights contradicts this as the Congress was prohibited from passing any law interfering with the right to peacefully assemble. Without protest though, we have sheepishly allowed court rulings to support the establishment of Exclusion Zones and Free Speech Zones, often located miles from the desired protest site and set behind concrete barriers, fencing, and razor wire.

Watching from a distance this past week I am concerned our government and media does not condemn Egypt's actions to shut down the internet and communications. With bi-partisan support the Senate is prepared to again introduce legislation to create an "Internet Kill Switch." In Egypt stopping communication has become necessary to thwart organizing by protesters. I believe many Americans view such actions as part of their perception of safety, but I counter it is another step in the incremental destruction of our freedoms. When challenged, a congressional white paper on the measure said the proposal prohibits the government from targeting websites for censorship "based solely on activities protected by the First Amendment of the United States Constitution." Ironically, the same language is used in the Patriot Act.

Our country is radically changing, not in terms of Democrat versus Republican, but government and corporations versus citizenry. Each of the Amendments of the Bill of Rights has been usurped over the last 40 years to protect the state and corporation. Meanwhile we have sat idly by accepting, like children, the supposed safety created in exchange for liberty. We have watched legislation pass that punishes minorities and the indigent in greater numbers. Currently the mainstream populace finds itself victim to the banking, mortgage, and credit fraud perpetrated by the elite few and legitimized by Congress. I challenge you to understand why youth in Egypt are risking their lives against oppression, question why Icelandic people rioted to avoid the indebtedness of the banks, why 170,000 TSA employees have the freedom to ignore the Fourth Amendment, and why both sides of Congress support legislation to cut communications via the Internet. From the comfort of our homes it is safer to let others protest and not put ourselves at risk. I think the answer to my wife's question about whether Americans riot is easy, "the passionate due, the idle don't."

Land of the Free (4/27/2011)

Our national anthem brings pride unto ourselves when we quote the famous lines, "O'er the land of the free and the home of the brave." Sadly, since that fateful night at Fort McHenry I would offer the founding fathers fight against royal tyranny for liberty and our forefathers shedding blood for future generations has been usurped by complacency. Examples abound in our current society of both the loss of freedom and lack of bravery.

A December 4, 2006 column in the Russian paper, Pravda, makes reference to "A record 7 million people - or one in every 32 American adults - were behind bars, on probation or on parole by the end of last year', and when these figures are added to the estimated 1 million prisoners of war held by the United States, all around the World, the once great American Nation has now become the greatest jailer of human beings the World has ever known." Laws such as "Three Strikes" have increased our incarceration rate for even the pettiest of crimes. Even the truly law-abiding are not free. Consider random traffic stops to check your license and insurance, TSA airport searches, security screenings to enter a public event, and proof of identity requirements for job applications and opening bank accounts. Exacerbating the situation is claims these freedoms are taken in the name of liberty.

Ironically, even bravery has been eroded out of fear of consequences. Questioning TSA regarding the 4th amendment and basis for searching six-year olds will prevent you from flying. Publicly videotaping law enforcement creates a fast path to court with criminal charges. My favorite example occurred two weeks ago: Juror 799, an Asian woman in her 20s, when asked to name three people she least admired on her juror questionnaire, wrote: "African-Americans, Hispanics and Haitians." In the land for the free and home of the brave the woman was sentenced to indefinite jury duty by Federal Judge Nicholas Garaufis – a unilateral decision with no crime committed.

I challenge you to listen carefully to political demagoguery and proposals to "make you safer." Blood was shed September 3, 1814 to capture freedom and liberty for future generations whilst Francis Scott Key watched the fight and immortalized his feelings. Sadly, our former enemies in Russia watch our freedoms erode and write about it, but the timidity bred into our generations of children makes them blind to the blood given for their liberty and they will not stand bravely for themselves.

iTracker (5/4/2011)

In the "Daily Mail" on 4/18/2011 I first read hackers in London discovered iPhones are recording and storing specific location data about their users. Initially the major networks and newspapers in America were slow to report this, taking almost 4 days to do so. Humorously Apple's, Steve Jobs first offered no such information was gathered and certainly without malicious intent. With persistence though, the media found more details and Jobs did acknowledge the data gathering. So what's my beef? As a programmer I do not consider the tracking file an accident and my concern is the potential misuse of the data. Possibly the programmers had good intentions but knowing a data record of individual details exists would be too tempting for use by others.

Let's consider three examples. First, police in Michigan have been accused of downloading the data during traffic stops, without warrants or arrest in violation of the 4th Amendment. Law enforcement could use the data to pinpoint the whereabouts of a particular individual. Imagine the phone doing detective work for the police by providing when and where he goes. Second, employees are at risk from employers as the employer typically owns the phone; thus the data can be checked to verify the whereabouts of employees to ensure he is working, or where reported during office hours. Third, consider a contested divorce with a vindictive ex-wife. Through Discovery the data file must be made available and the husband's whereabouts at any time readily known. In my second and third examples the 4th Amendment does not apply, thus anyone with an iPhone has already voluntarily submitted to 24-hour tracking.

My preference is to believe Apple had no malicious intent in mind when the file was created and most likely it was created to improve location data services and their product service offering. However, some have reported this is a requirement under the Telecommunications Act of 1996 and most likely "we the people" allowed this further erosion of our privacy and personal rights to take place based on the premise, "they would never do anything bad and it will help stop crime or save lives." In my recent column, "Land of the Free" I argued there is no longer bravery among us and we idly standby while our freedoms disappear. Personally, I have deleted the file on my phone and will continue to do so. Maybe it still exists on a server somewhere, but at least I have fought back. My concern is when will anyone else fight back?

Gestapo and Gulags (6/15/2011)

Congress successfully reauthorized the Patriot Act on May 27th, 2011 with hours remaining before the Act would expire. America is eerily following the same path Hitler's Nazi Germany took in the early 1930's; a path of Federal law enforcement, diminished civil rights, and lack of transparency in the courts. The Gestapo was given the authority to investigate treason, espionage, sabotage and criminal attacks against Germany. The basic law passed in 1936 gave the Gestapo the right to operate without judicial oversight. The Gestapo could not be sued by citizens in Administrative court.

Americans are subjecting themselves to our own Gestapo, Department of Homeland Security (DHS) willfully. Examples abound from TSA searches, disrobement, and groping at airports, rail stations, and even high school proms to document and papers required to open a bank account or get a job. Openly over the last 18 years there has been a push from local community law enforcement to a federally dominated model of control. Any local assertion of state's power is met with federal resistance, like the Arizona and Georgia immigration lawsuits or economic threats to Texas over passing an anti-groping bill. DHS has pushed a "see something, say something" campaign to encourage spying on neighbors and standing up to Big Brother is now cause for consideration as "domestic terrorist." It was that "domestic terrorism" that brought us freedom and the genesis of our country.

As police power expands, and 1st, 2nd, and 4th Amendment rights are reduced more citizens are being jailed than ever before. The term "Gulag" was originally an acronym for the Soviet agency administering the prisons, but has since come to represent any penal system. America has sharply turned her view on incarceration from one of rehabilitation to mandate. In 1982 approximately 1 of 77 Americans was under "correctional-control", today that number is 1 of 31. Georgia leads the country with 1 of 13 adults under some type of judicial supervision. Take into account wage garnishment orders, child support orders, and foreclosure liens and judicial findings and the number is higher. Today the United States has the highest incarceration rate (3.1%) and the largest prison population of any country in the world. Even communist China with three times the population incarcerates fewer people.

The trend I see developing is one of government control creating fear among the citizens. I challenge you, "what consequences would you face if you question how TSA handles you?" What would you expect to happen if you say "no" to a police officer regarding a roadside search? Why are our countryman arrested for filming police stops? Why do victimless crimes, like drug use or possession, result in incarceration? More frequently the noose is tightening around our necks, "We the People.."

Defending Yourself (06/22/2011)

I wrestled with the title and content of this column realizing I wanted to challenge thought processes. My context is asking, "When would you take up arms?" Recent Supreme Court rulings, at state level and the federal level have eroded 4th Amendment rights. These freedoms have been held sacred since the Bill of Rights passed and evolved from British tyranny and further back to feudal tyranny. Looking around I see this erosion becoming the norm, no longer the exception. Sadly, people who raise questions are now "domestic terrorists" or "troublemakers" harassed through detention, no-fly lists, and watch lists.

If you are pulled aside for additional screening at an airport and suddenly find yourself touched inappropriately by a TSA officer are you willing to yell "Stop!" Are you willing to kick and punch to defend your person? Are you willing to engage local law enforcement to file assault charges? What if you are an 18 year old girl attending your high school prom and security guards run a hand up your bare thigh under your dress? Would you be willing to complain, or more importantly file a lawsuit like Candice Herrara of Santa Fe, New Mexico?

Examples of concern abound. Recent state and federal Supreme Court rulings have changed search and seizure rules allowing police offers more leeway. My question, without cause and absolutely wrong in your view and demanding entry to your home would you let them in? Similarly, what if you are legally and rightfully openly carrying a gun and police officers, not knowing the law, are now threatening you at gunpoint and moving to arrest you, as recently occurred in Philadelphia? What if you were selling unpasteurized milk or free range eggs on your farm and USDA Officials raided your homestead, guns drawn, and arrested you even though no crime was committed.

In theory we are all safe in our homes, our cars, and while traveling. Our founding fathers experienced British tyranny and knew fundamentally they had to protect themselves, their families, and their property. Obsequious citizenry today is leading to a government police state that turns neighbors against each other and infallible beliefs in lawmakers. Sooner or later "Dancing with Stars" will end and a confused America will realize they lost the freedom to defend themselves. Our children will believe pat-downs to attend prom are the norm and police can enter homes anytime. Are you willing to speak up and defend yourself? "The truth is that all men having power ought to be mistrusted," James Madison.

6 ECONOMIC COLLAPSE

Snowstorms (2/17/2010)

The last several weeks living in North Georgia have made me long for the warm weather of New Smyrna. Snow has fallen across the mountains and into the Mid-Atlantic States. Mentioned in the news, but not garnering huge attention, has been the concern over budget shortfalls to handle snow removal and storm effects. The next economic storm brewing is more significant than this winter's snowstorms though, it is the budget shortfalls at city, county, and state levels. Unlike the Federal government the other levels of government cannot run deficit budgets, leaving IOUs, payment vouchers, and possible insolvency as their only options.

Currently, California's state budget is $40 billion, and assumes $9.6 billion in revenue will come from the Federal government, although it is rumored unlikely. Watching the news, the "Governator" remains firm on passing budgets, leaving programs intact, and not raising taxes. Sadly, Arnold has been at the front of the line grabbing monies for his state, in sharp contrast to what most Republican governors tend to do. Along with California; Illinois, Arizona, Florida, Michigan, Nevada, New Jersey, Oregon, Rhode Island and Wisconsin are also on the verge of fiscal disaster. Each of these states shares in common an increase in spending to fund public pension plans and support social programs that outpaced revenues. Coupled with the economic downturn, and housing crisis, revenues have fallen sharply. States like Arizona and Florida saw legislators enjoy spending due to property tax growth and found themselves like giddy children with an unlimited budget in a toy store full of opportunity.

Compounding the state problems are unfunded pension liabilities. Teachers, firefighters, policemen, and other public service employees enjoy an opportunity that allows productive members of society to work a limited number of years and then retire. In California the projected teacher pension shortfall is currently $43 billion, a huge number that can only be made up through taxes, additional contributions, or reduced benefits.

At the municipal level, foreclosures have created property tax deficits and reduced spending has cut sales tax revenues. Adding to revenue problems, and wiping out reserves, is increased expense for snowstorms, ice storms, and potential hurricanes this summer. "*USA Today*" ran an article on February 3rd, 2010 examining road maintenance under the caption, "Tight times put gravel on the road." The article noted gravel roads are emerging as a sign of financial struggle in rural towns. In this case, budgets are so constrained that regular maintenance can no longer be performed on asphalt roads, something we all take for granted. Additionally, we have seen the fantastic examples of bridge failures, and can expect more infrastructure failures of roads, sewer, and water.

Listening to a podcast during the last week the discussion turned to the economy and the participants talked about local insolvencies, and mortgage resets, making an observation, "if it were really that bad wouldn't someone tell us?" In hindsight, no warnings were given leading to the housing bust, or the market crash in March 2009. Looking back further, the headlines of the 1930's are hilarious with weekly pontifications of better times coming and I believe our economic recovery is going to echo a similar path. I realize that comment contradicts the optimistic news presented daily. However too many factors remain: unemployment, reduced tax revenues, drains on local spending, excessive quantitative easing, Chinese currency manipulation, and increased spending. It seems like Americans have become the proverbial frog in a pot of hot water, slowly being boiled to death, oblivious to the impending doom.

The Good Old Days (3/17/2010)

In my lifetime I never thought I would refer to "when times were good", or "the good old days," terms I always thought were left to my grandparents. Of course, some life experience is required before such a reference can be made and this might also mean I am getting older. Without a doubt we can now have conversations that start with the statement, "when times were good" and instantly pinpoint a reference we all understand. Curiously, when riding the euphoria of economic success it is easy to ignore the impending potential crash. Although the one year anniversary of the stock market low was just last week, it was the peak of November 2007 that defines the tombstone of good times. Since then personal experience through home loss, job loss, bankruptcy, asset sales, and moving have defined America. Most of us know someone touched by the recession and we will forever be influenced by what is happening around us.

Just recently I have been in several conversations where the words "when times were good" were stated. The first time I paused momentarily, but everyone present understood what was said. The next day the same scenario similarly repeated itself and I realized something important had happened. Essentially, the most recent economic downturn has cemented in our minds a change and we are living through a time which only the rearview mirror of history will provide a true opinion. Unlike Pearl Harbor Day or September 11th, it will take years to understand the Great Recession of 2008-2010. Although hardships are upon many Americans, a theme of ignoring main street has developed.

Looking at history of the Great Depression of the 1930s brings similar observations. For example, 1930 and 1931 provide numerous examples of President Hoover and Treasury Secretary Andrew Mellon assuring the people the worst was over and prosperity was right around the corner. In a May 1, 1930 statement, Hoover said, "*While the crash only took place six months ago, I am convinced we have now passed the worst and with continued unity of effort we shall rapidly recover. There is one certainty of the future of a people of the resources, intelligence and character of the people of the United States - that is, prosperity.*"

History has an uncanny ability to repeat itself, but yet we fail to learn from our experiences. At one level those living in the government and financial centers of our country seem to enjoy uncontrolled spending, record deficits, market highs, profits, and record bonuses. For the rest of us, business closings, vacant office space, abandoned homes, increasing food and fuel costs, and unemployment seem to be the norm. *"I see no reason why 1931 should not be an extremely good year."* - Alfred P. Sloan, Jr. of General Motors Co. stated in November 1930. Week after week we see conflicting economic news streaming at us, reports of increased consumer spending for February indicate despite snowstorms we reached in our pockets to spend money, but contradictorily consumer sentiment dropped.

My point is we have to wonder how the current economic environment will shape our own lives and futures. Our children may never know "when times were good" if our economy stagnates like the 1930s. My confidence in massive spending at levels never before seen is low, because there are always consequences to every action. Future generations will have to pay for this administration's actions either through taxes or inflation as there is no other way to slow the velocity of increase in the money supply. A cloud hangs over our economy and future; I wish things were like "the good old days."

Ripple Effects (6/2/2010)

Off the beaten path and traveling the back roads of the countryside brings opportunity to cross paths with new people. Recently passing through a small town I struck up conversation with the proprietor of a local service station and I commented on the lumber mill and how fortunate the town was to have industry. My new friend then informed me the mill had just closed, permanently, two weeks before after 100 years in business. Over 1,100 jobs were lost at the mill, but the real tragedy he said "was the ripple effect." He explained there were house cleaners, landscape companies, automobile service garages, pressure washers, and even the local dry cleaner that depended on the employees of the mill to buy their services.

In conversation another friend shared with me the story of the recession on an aviation business, losing fuel sales due to the cutback of medical transplant flights. Curious, I asked why and learned the typical transplant donor is a male, aged 18-24 who dies in a motorcycle crash. In this recession those young males cannot buy motorcycles due to the credit crisis. Therefore due to the economy there is no credit, no motorcycle purchases, no crashes, no transplants, no flights, and no sales.

Since 2007 the economy has struggled to regain footing, slowed down like a marathon runner in the 18th mile. Restarting the economic engine is more serious than easing credit, encouraging spending, or building confidence. The concept of the "new normal" which mirrors Europe's economy with high unemployment, social programs to help those in need, and lackluster performance is cheered as a political success. In this recession two very different demographics have suffered catastrophically: low-income minorities on one end and high-income whites on the other. Expecting to find themselves in the most prosperous years of their lives the 40-55 year old group of white males has learned the jobs they once coveted have been shipped off-shore, gone forever. Cities like Detroit are facing 50% unemployment, arguably far from an economic recovery. Regardless of which group is examined though, it is apparent society has been slow to understand this change. If not unemployed, then a blind eye is turned to those who need help with housing, loans, child support, and groceries.

Movies like the "Butterfly Effect" or stories like Ray Bradbury's "A Sound of Thunder" exemplify the catastrophic possibilities of small changes to once known realities. In 2010 we are experiencing the ripple effects of radical changes to a once vibrant economic system. As of this month more Americans than any time in history receive food stamps, nearly 40 million, real unemployment according to a recent Gallup poll is close to 20%, and the housing market is set to fall again due to the end of government tax incentives. I must agree with the words, "new normal" and assert our success will depend on adaptability, not returning to what we once had.

Economic Recovery? (9/1/2010)

Last week Vice President Joe Biden took credit for the economic recovery underway. I disagree based on facts. First, the unemployment rate is 2-3 points worse than projected without a stimulus package. Second, four important housing numbers last week illustrate no recovery: existing home sales fell 27% over the prior month to a historic low, new home sales fell to the lowest number since 1963, existing home inventories rose to a historic level, and interest rates fell to a historic low. Third, the teen jobless rate is at the lowest level since 1948. Fourth, the GDP was revised downward for the second quarter by approximately 30%, thus deflating the optimism the already sluggish number was a sign of recovery. Fifth, the ratio of job seekers to jobs remains high at 5:1 versus historic averages.

In December 2008 I wrote a seven page paper detailing my predictions for the economy after the presidential election. One friend poked fun saying I had written my "manifesto" while away in the mountains. Interestingly, I re-read the paper before last week's numbers came out and my predictions were prophetic. If we disregard the stock market, I accurately predicted any lack of recovery. In hindsight though, main street does not care about the Dow Jones 30 Industrials, nor should they. The pundits of financial television spoke of "green shoots" and pontificated recovery for the last twelve months while working Americans have lost jobs, homes, and credit. Concurrently, bankers subsidized by TARP have profited handsomely.

The biggest problem in measuring this recovery is the data itself. The DJIA changes, and has changed since the crash in March 2009. Thus, this index of companies is not the same index it was in the 1930s, or even 18 months ago. Second, the government has changed its methods of measuring inflation and unemployment. Our 9.6% unemployment rate, indicating we are in better condition than the Great Depression, is closer to 20% when measured the way unemployment was reported in the 1930s.

I therefore assert we are in a "Hidden Depression". There are no soup lines, but 40.3 million Americans receive food stamps. Unemployment benefits have been extended to protect families. Unlike the 1930s, we own more "stuff" and it appears to protect our personal falls. Sadly, our leaders are repeating the failings of the Great Depression: providing false optimism, ignoring main street and rewarding banks, and implementing policies doomed to failure.

Bob Cratchit (12/22/2010)

Without much thought most of us can recite the plot of Dicken's *A Christmas Carol* and the various scenes of ghostly Jacob Marley torturing the soul of Ebenezer Scrooge. Dicken's indictment of 19th century capitalism is just as accurate 167 years after publication. Although in denial, most Americans have more in common with the hurting Bob Cratchit and family than the wealthy, out of touch Ebenezer Scrooge this Christmas.

I challenge you to consider how your Christmas four years ago compares to this year and what concerns are facing you, your family, friends, and our country. Christmas 2006 we had never heard of candidate Barak Obama, the national debt was 8.5 trillion versus 14 trillion today, 258 U.S. soldiers had died in Afghanistan versus 1437 total through today, and unemployment was 4.6% compared to the current 9.8% with over 8 million jobs lost in just the last two years. Personally, Christmas 2006 was incredible as my house was "worth" far more than I had paid, and I was a believer in the infinitely upward movement of American economic growth. Two years of unemployment wiped out my entire career's worth of wealth building. Regardless of your opinion of the financial crisis, our political parties, or presidential administrations this Christmas is different.

Last week at Wal-Mart my wife spoke to a cashier who had her heat fail and was using space heaters to warm her home. With their 3-year old sharing a bed to stay warm she said the house dropped to the same temperature as outdoors, 15°F. I assert most of us are like Bob Cratchit, just surviving to stay warm and struggling to feed our families. The debt crazed, home equity financed Christmas is now the Ghost of Christmas Past. This year the Ghost of Christ Present has brought prudence, fear, and common sense upon America. State employees, teachers, and educated engineers and managers wonder if tomorrow will bring a pink slip or another week of toiling hours just to keep a job, unappreciated by the likes of Scrooge. Bankers however will bask with overgrown golden turkeys, excesses of food and thermostats set at 74 °F unlike 60 °F for the common folk. And what about the third specter? The Ghost of Christmas Yet to Come will more than likely deliver further pain and woe to already hurting families. "When people lose everything and they have nothing to lose, they lose it." - Gerald Celente

1970s versus 201Xs

The kids wearing plaid pants and striped shirts with long hair watching the "*Brady Bunch*", "*Adam-12*" and "*Emergency*" are the men and women running our government today. It seems these "kids" have no recollection of the politics or monetary policy of the 1970s, instead only remembering the Bicentennial, bell bottom jeans, and Nerf footballs. A careful examination will show a decade that suffered an energy crisis causing an immediate recession. The same happened in 2008 when oil prices rose rapidly to $147/bbl driving our economy over a cliff to financial Armageddon. Nixon removed the Gold standard in 1971, and the Federal Reserve enacted new monetary policies to bring recovery. No radical method helped Nixon or Ford, and a hopeless Democrat was elected; promising prosperity and unable to deliver as we added the word "stagflation" to our vocabulary. As America entered the 1980s, after seven years of lackluster growth interest rates rose rapidly crushing the housing recovery. I remember my own parents struggling with 18% rates, job loss, and our manufacturing shift overseas as Chrysler sought a bailout and American's learned "Made in Japan" meant quality compared to our union produced assembly lines.

For ten years inflation was high, reaching 13.5% in 1980 and unemployment soared above 10%, but like today the same policies were held: Federal spending never slowed, and tax increases for the rich were proposed. Gold prices accelerated and fueled speculation the end was near and the economy would not survive. Talk of wind mills, solar panels, energy conservation, and self-sufficiency abounded. Reviewing newspapers from the early 1980's it is easy to spot Tip O'Neill's 100-plus Democrat majority was adding to federal spending faster than the revenues received, not unlike the recent Pelosi dynasty. I found one article stating for every 1% increase in unemployment Federal spending deficits increased by $25-40 billion during the 1982 recession because unemployment drives down revenue and causes government to spend more.

Many argue the cornucopianism of Ronald Reagan saved the economy through supply-side tax cuts. I would argue a direct correlation should be made between recovery and oil prices as the UK's discoveries of North Sea oil increased supply and probably fueled the recovery of the 1980's and 1990's. The 1970's are remembered for Disco and parties, instead we should truly understand the damage of failed economic policies. We are three years into the current economic decline and the kids I knew now run Congress; I would offer 1970's history provides more answers than the academic speculation used today.

Wisconsin (2/23/2011)

I debated whether to offer an opinion regarding Wisconsin, but knew I could not let go of this protest. I am impressed with the 65,000 plus protesters that believe in something strong enough to brave the cold. More important to see debate with such passion engaging on our own soil gives me hope toward future revolution against our government and tyranny we face. It appears the press – from the left and right, have managed to blur the issue at hand as there only appears two possible opposing views when tapping MSNBC or Fox News. I hypothesize three parties are now at war in this country: Public Servants, the Ruling Elite (executive pay), and the Private Sector. Thus, a two pointed perspective does not work and furthermore the issue at hand is not about trimming union rights, but re-aligning public servant compensation.

Austerity measures will generate class warfare and in this Great Recession the compensation of the three parties has diverged greatly. Executive pay remained safe and increased greatly and Public Service payrolls have increased far greater than private payrolls. On the other hand, the Private Sector has suffered irreplaceable job losses, flat wages and lives in fear of a pink slip delivery tomorrow. At the same time the Private Sector is asked to pay more income tax, more sales tax, more property tax, and more fees to pay for the perpetuation of Public Service compensation programs and to bailout reckless executives who lost gambling bets against the masses during the debt fueled frenzy.

Ancient Rome succeeded through an ever expanding territorial economy fueling the wants and desires of Caesar. The masses found relief through entertainment at the Coliseum and a sense of safety, but yet traded liberty for trite compensation. Similarly, America is like Rome; rich Senators, a small ruling class, and wealth obtained for a few due to the destruction of others. Our masses are entertained by media and sports, not taking time to understand the reason behind the need for change. Like Rome our public servants are protected by a never ending spigot of tax dollars and turn against the working class and income earners for whom they supposedly serve.

It is forgotten that our children will ultimately pay the price. Something is happening in America right now, and it started with the bursting of the debt bubble three years ago. Denial has not worked and protests will become more common, maybe leading to revolution. I am concerned for my children's future and cannot imagine the tax burden, inflation, and tyranny they will face if we do not stop oppose the protesters in Wisconsin.

Destroying Futures (3/2/2011)

Imagine earning $30,000 (3 Trillion) per year but having bills and obligations of $42,000 (4.2 Trillion) per year. Additionally, let's assume you have a spouse and two children with wants and desires. With your income falling short you would know radical changes in your lifestyle must be made and if you are a Dave Ramsey fan you know every expenditure would have to be considered and nearly one-fourth must be cut. However, the kids will complain if you cut their movies, food, school activities, clothes and even iTunes budget (government spending). Your spouse does not want to discuss the issue because she feels the problem will go away, as if by magic, and there is no reason to upset the kids (political debate).

However, there is an answer: debt. Of course, a loan to create a source of "income" can be created (deficit spending). For instance, a second mortgage on your home could fund the shortfall and maybe allow you to buy a new big-screen television or car, a hugely popular decision at home. But this only works for a while, quickly you discover the interest only payments add another $500 per month to your obligations, thus you are now using the debt taken on to pay for the original shortfall and the new debt (treasury auctions)! You have looked for ways to increase income, but the economy isn't growing and no one is hiring (tax revenue). Your anxiety increases because you know this cannot keep going and bankruptcy may be the only way out.

One day however, your neighbor Fred (Federal Reserve) knocks on your door and explains his multi-level marketing business is doing well and along as he keeps getting new people involved his success will grow and he would like to help you. Hesitantly you agree to his proposal: he will paper over your debt (purchase bonds), and you can repay him in 30-years. Thoughtfully you think his proposed near zero interest rate and 30-year offer has to work. At age 50 it is even unlikely you will be here in 30 years to deal with the repercussions. With a wink, Fred explains your children will assume the entire debt, with interest. After contemplation you feel it is better to risk your children's future than to reign in your lifestyle today, and hurt their feelings, and since they do not get an opinion (can't vote) they will never know. Like a deal with the devil, you know there is no way out.

Dad's Money (2/23/2010)

Nightly we are bombarded by incomprehensible numbers regarding Federal government spending: $14 trillion debt, $4 trillion budget, $1.5 trillion deficit and $180 billion interest payments. There are too many zeros on each number to print in this column, twelve each for the debt and deficit. Sadly, like gamblers in Las Vegas using colored poker chips we have lost sight of reality because no one touches the monies. As taxpayers our view of the government has become like a child's view of Dad's spending. A five-year-old watching his father has no idea where he gets money, but feels there is an endless supply. Sometimes Dad reaches in his pocket and uses green currency or coins like nickels and pennies. Other times Dad uses colorful plastic cards and swipes them in machines, and Dad has a book with checks where he illegibly scribbles names and amounts and declares the bills are paid. Of course, he also logs on his computer and banks via the web. Similarly, the government engages in a playful deception of payments, using computers, checks, and cash cards to move monies around.

Dad always seems to have money and as five-year olds we know he leaves each day and goes to work to make more. A connection between work and money seems obvious because doing chores sometimes brings allowance to children. As young children we always seem to have food, clothes, and toys. We don't know how the lights operate or anything about mortgages and rent, insurance, gasoline, or car payments. However, we know dad takes care of us and most citizens view the government the same way with no understanding of tax income or expenditures

Right now we are enjoying historically low interest rates, easing interest payments on our $14 trillion debt. If interest rates return to historic norms of 6% the payments will increase to approximately $840 billion, nearly 23% of our current budget. Like a five -year-old trusting Dad to make money and spend money to care for the family we believe our elected trustees will do the same. However, re-election drives decision making, not the tough longevity of parenting and sadly our federal government is recklessly spending money. Congress must be held accountable for the deficit spending because they are bankrupting our country. Every parent and grandparent should know what is happening and encourage Congress to stop today's fiscal negligence. Congress is punishing our future generations with inflation, high interest rates and more taxes. Sadly a five-year-old cannot stop Dad's recklessness, but as a voter you can stop Congress.

I Am Angry (3/23/2011)

I am angry because it appears no one knows what is going on around them with deficits, rising fuel prices, Islamic radicalization, and Middle East uprising. The most twisted issue is an American society willing to tax food, clothing, and shelter and support 44 million Americans on food stamps while watching media celebrities like Charlie Sheen make fools of themselves. It cost an extra "Andrew Jackson" to fill my car today and the mainstream blames fuel prices on the Middle East, but that's far from the truth. A middle-school look at the readily available data shows a more fundamental reason for the rise, one destroying our lifestyle and future.

Rising fuel prices are simply attributed to three factors: monetary supply, supply and demand, and speculation. Speculation is based on fear in the market which is driven by political unrest around the world. Supply and demand is a direct consequence of emerging economies, hurricanes in the Gulf, or destruction of Middle East oil assets. Although the Middle East uprisings are dominating news reports daily, the current rising prices are truly a function of monetary supply. Fed Chairman Ben Bernanke speculated on QE2 in August 2010 and it was officially announced November 4, 2010. Each week I graph crude oil prices and up until August prices were relatively stable, but immediately following QE2's speculation fuel prices started to rise, increasing more after the official announcement. With the devaluation of our currency, OPEC announced a desire for higher fuel prices to effectively capture the same income. Today's Middle Eastern uprising is a secondary issue exacerbating the underlying cause of rising fuel prices. Blame our government and central bank, not those fighting for civil liberties.

The solutions being thrown around by political pundits from both sides make no sense and demonstrate politics' need-to-please, not realistic solutions. Opening strategic reserves is anecdotal to a giving a cancer patient a band-aid. *The Long Emergency*, as James Howard Kunstler writes, has begun and political unrest, failed monetary policies, and a third-world desirous of the same excesses we enjoy will continue to drive oil prices upward. I am angry pop-culture nonsense Tom Brady's hair and Gaga's breast milk ice cream exploits resonates more importantly than the collapse of our currency. On November 10, 2010 I wrote, "Gasoline should easily reach $3.40/gallon by April as OPEC is demanding a minimum $100/gallon." I am angry no one listens.

The Hydra Monster (4/13/2011)

On Friday Americans will repeat the annual ritual of paying taxes. Local television stations will provide live coverage from postal offices near closing time; editorializing what we "must" do to pay our taxes. Obediently most all of her citizens will have complied and the monster of government will continue living, and regardless of attack she cannot be killed through starvation or even radical cuts. Valiantly some men are trying like Congressmen Ron Paul and Paul Ryan, but attempts to shut down the government and truly kill the monster to save future generations are met with mockery from the press and she continues to live.

Sadly, the Hydra Monster lives at all levels of our lives. We start with our paychecks by enslaving ourselves for the first three to four months of the year to pay Federal income tax (20%) and FICA (7.65%). Sadly, most people ignore the 7.65% raise they would receive if employers did not have to pay taxes "on their behalf." In Georgia I have a state tax of approximately 3% and there are the other taxes my employer pays instead of paying me: SUTA and FUTA. Adding it all together nearly 40% of our paycheck is gone. In November most local municipalities seek property taxes on those who own real estate, amounts of $5-$15k are averages in Volusia County (let's assume 10% of income). With every purchase comes sales tax: 6.5%. Adding everything together comes to 55% of earnings. Of course, there are countless fees and taxes on phones, internet, licenses, and registrations further driving up costs.

Taxes anger me because the Hydra Monster called government relentlessly feeds itself on the backs of all men and abusively spends the collected monies. At the national level the monster is so large the President readily acknowledged during his promotion of healthcare fraud and waste in Medicare comes to $1 billion, but the monster lives on. Locally governments build multi-million dollar firehouses on prime commercial property and create pension plans to allow productive citizens to withdraw from the workforce at early ages. In Nassau County, NY policeman earn $100k after five years and are entitled to hundreds of thousands in annual retirement benefits!

Our country is dying, consumed by the Hydra Monster. No matter how hard our heroes try to cut a head she will live on, breathing fire against her people, growing meaninglessly, and adding more heads to become ever more pervasive and invasive in our lives. Radical change is required to defeat the Hydra Monster, only banded together can she be killed. Paying taxes this week is a sad offering to the misery befalls man but will make the Monster stronger.

The King's Speech (04/20/2011)

I have never been as angry after a President's speech as I was last week. Being forthright, I do not like Obama, never have, and never will. I believe he was unqualified to lead our country, has blamed others for his failures, will not hold himself accountable, and ultimately we disagree on the direction our country should go. Furthermore, I believe the Republicans have nothing different to offer than to protect their own interests and continue stealing our freedoms.

The King had an opportunity to win the American people over to the proposals for our future. Our fiscal situation is dire, inflation is increasing, wages are falling, energy and food prices are increasing, the Democrats have proposed spending $1.4

trillion more than tax revenues will produce, and in just 2 years the King and his court have increased the national debt 33%. The Jester, John Boehner, bragged regarding the bipartisan budget agreement, largest in history, but that lie only survived a week. The CBO reported the "real" cuts are only $352 million, less than 1% of the lie put to us.

The King, Jester, court, and sleeping beauty (Joe Biden) know how government works; let me explain. Let's say you and I spend $100/month on eating out and decide next month we will budget $50 more dollars for dining. Using government accounting if we reduce the total budget to $120, we "saved" $30! There were no cuts; we just didn't spend what we planned to, unlike spending $70 you and I would have inferred. Because my children's future is in peril let me propose true government responsibility: mandatory 15% income tax for everyone, 20% for all corporations, and reducing the tax code to just one page as there will be no deductions of any kind. Second, eliminate the Departments of Energy, Education, Interior, Homeland Security, and Health and Human Services. Third, close all foreign military bases. Fourth, eliminate public funding of arts, Planned Parenthood, charitable programs, and any constitutionally questionable program. Fifth, cut all Congressional member and staff budgets and salaries by 50%. Sixth, eliminate all civil service pension plans and special medical plans. Seventh, remind our elderly that Social Security and Medicare were supplemental programs, not entitlements, and cut the monthly benefit to $750/person, regardless of income or marriage.

Only radical, truthful proposals will work to save our country. A parent makes tough decisions and redirects behavior; similarly we need politicians to lead, not steal our futures. The current tomfoolery will continue to strengthen the uprising and anger in America and revolution against the elected royalty will occur.

Wealth Disparity (5/11/2011)

A drive through New Smyrna Beach demonstrates the extreme wealth disparity that can be found anywhere in America or the world. From the mega-wealth of beachside to the barely surviving poor west of U.S. Highway 1 radical contrasts in daily life are found. It is impossible to look away in a small town and not acknowledge differences, to ignore them would be unconscionable. Like New Smyrna, America's numbers are mind-blowing: the top 1% controls nearly 33% of the wealth in America whereas the bottom 50% has just 2.5% of the wealth.

Don't misunderstand me. I love nice things, eating out, a beautiful home, new cars, and a big bank account. As a country even our poorest live far better than the middle class does overseas, but such argument is not cause for turning our backs on the needy. Similarly, the populist envy driven by our current President does not justify excessively taxing wage earners, or the ultra-wealthy. The current raging debate has disclosed the failures of our progressive tax system: envy that the "rich" pay much of their tax through a 15% dividend, and sadly uncovering through subsidies and support programs a single mother of three earning $14,000 per year has more disposable income than a similar mother earning $60,000.

We need the successful to succeed, creating jobs, opportunities, and capital for driving the economy. Simultaneously an understanding and empathy must exist for those who need help. I do not have solutions, but must argue the debate is lost in political rhetoric and desire to drive pet projects. Taxing the wealthy at 100% will not provide enough revenue to fix the government spending problem and it certainly will not lift those in need. Milton Friedman argues in the movie, "The One Percent" the increasing wealth gap is justified because it has also lifted the poorest of poor. In earlier lectures Friedman, in characteristic fashion, shows at least that government creates a perverse system starting with bad schools, limits opportunity through minimum wage laws, and creates dependency via welfare programs.

The political debate from both sides focuses on our tax system and protecting special interests, Republicans arguing to keep tax rates low on the rich, Democrats seeking more. Sadly, both sides view 67,000 pages of tax code as the holy grail of government purpose and fail to understand simplifying the tax system and cutting spending will allow market forces to work toward solutions benefitting both rich and poor.

Small Town Destruction (7/13/2011)

In my job I drive through small towns throughout the southeast U.S. It saddens me to see these former, vibrant communities withering away. Most people would find easy reasons for the local downfalls, like manufacturing plants closing. There is some truth to this, and of course the long-term trends in demographics point toward moves toward the suburbs, but I would argue the root cause is the locally self destructive historic actions of the communities themselves. I believe there are three distinct errors.

First, "we need a bypass." One can follow US441, US301, or US1 in Georgia and Florida to see numerous examples. Beautiful towns are bypassed by high speed highways giving no reason to slow and take a look. The land on the bypass is commercialized by modern developers building look-a-like cheap structures found anywhere in America. The unique downtown charm of Main Street is then left to die. Ironically, my Garmin GPS has routed me through many towns, instead of the bypass, as the shorter faster route. I have enjoyed this scenic discovery and reminder of small town charm, and enjoy the scenery of the plantation homes, brick buildings, and unique architecture versus the lackluster appearance of the bypass.

Second, "we need a national retailer." Too often a local lobby to bring a national big box store to town under the guise of job creation turns into job shift and tax incentives amounting to bribery. Sadly, locally spent dollars give way to money transfer outside the local economy. Given the option between a national retailer and a local merchant, most consumers will choose the big store. The Main Street hardware, grocery or auto repair store, where they know your name, is wiped out by the faceless corporation. Of course, the box store provides amenities like longer hours and opening Sundays, but the minimum wage employees don't know the products, customer names, or industry in which they are selling.

Third, "we can't have alcohol sales." Respectfully the values of the conservative South must give way to allow beer and wine sales at local restaurants. The primary revenue stream for restaurants is drinks: soda and tea for $2.00, beer and wine for as much as $5.00 a glass. Without this joyful elixir food choices are not gourmet, but relegated to diner-style, low-end choices forcing consumers to look for other options. My preference would be the locally-owned unique establishment with an atmosphere conducive for business or a romantic evening. These establishments spawn the growth of nearby merchants because there is now a reason to be downtown.

Our own town of Cleveland, Georgia is facing tough decisions, but it appears the local political establishment has opened themselves to public opinion. Next time you travel I encourage you to avoid the highway and take a trip through the nearby small towns. Avoid the bypass; choose the "business" route. Don't eat at a national chain, but find a local restaurant. If you need something, stop at a local merchant, not a national box store. The recipe for success is not difficult, but sadly undoing the prior destruction, or motions set in place, is nearly impossible.

Small Town Destruction – Part II (7/20/2011)

In my first column addressing the demise of small towns I pinpointed three items I believe are consistent in the recipe for disaster: highway bypasses taking traffic around town, national retailers undermining local merchants, and outdated alcohol ordinances preventing thriving dining. Objective and specific, I believe the slow withering of communities can be avoided and in no way do I question the emotional appeal of charm or the fabric of the community. Expanding further on the recipe to create sustainability several more key strategies, in addition to the original three, can be implemented.

First, tax policy can drive business toward town center through a reverse property tax or by creating community redevelopment districts. Traditionally property taxes are lower in the suburbs, by reversing the millage rate growth is encouraged toward town and away from the outskirts.

Second, mixed-use and re-use are critical to a thriving downtown. For example, a national drugstore or bookstore may come to town, but in place of a new steel and concrete structure replicated nationwide, require use of existing buildings and rehabilitation. As an avid fan of James Howard Kunstler, I must agree with his descriptions of "programming" the content inside the building versus the "container" that makes up the structure. A drugstore could operate from a 100-year old building, thus preserving the unique character of individual towns. Mixed-use and appropriate zoning would allow shopkeepers, or tenants, to live above shops in town center increasing rent and covering fixed costs for the building owner.

Third, discretionary consumerism should be incidental to the town center, not the primary focus. In a struggling economy counting on the luxury purchase of boutique goods will not save businesses. I propose keeping banking, postal, personal care, hardware, and grocery near town center instead of spreading these key needs to faceless strip malls located in yet to be developed suburbs. Consuming luxuries will follow naturally in a shopping district providing necessities.

Lastly, zoning and permit approvals should look toward the future by asking what will be left of this "container" if the business closes or moves. For example one national retailer is notorious for abandoning functional stores strongly anchoring numerous small businesses in favor of trading up to a generic "superstore" version located on cheaper land and incentivized by property tax reductions. Once left behind no other business is capable of using the commercial square footage and the nearby businesses that benefitted from the anchor fold, vandalism grows, and the entire shopping center becomes a permanent blight on the community.

Driving through the rural southeast I see success and failure from the window of my car. A thriving community is easily observed versus the shuttered, empty storefronts of a now dead town. I can't stop and ask about the "charm" or the "fabric" of the community, but I can see the faces of those pondering what happened and why the town died compared to the success of the community next door.

Collapse is Starting (8/10/2011)

President Obama promised "Hope and Change" when he was elected; he has definitely managed to deliver "Change," and last week he was quoted saying "Hope" doesn't happen overnight. Change has come at us like a freight train and repeatedly I have our covered loss of civil liberties, now our economic future has been stolen by Washington:

The debt deal promised cuts, but the debt will increase by $8 trillion dollars to $23 trillion by 2021. "Why?" Because the government calls a "cut" less spending than was projected for the following year, not less than is spent now.

The day after the deal passed the government spent $236 billion, or $750 per citizen, in a single day. For my family of six, the debt increased by $4500. I don't have an extra $4500 lying around, do you?

- Standard and Poor's downgraded the U.S. credit outlook for the first time in history on August 5, 2011. To claim this is a political move would underscore the objectivity of credit reporting.
- The official Chinese news agency commented, "China has every right now to demand the United States address its structural debt problems and ensure the safety of China's dollar assets."

- Food stamp usage hit a new historic high last week, 45.5 million, up from 26 million in January 2007, and 32 million in January 2009 when Obama took office.
- According to the Census Bureau, homeownership fell to the lowest level since 1998, 65.9%, and if delinquencies are included the numbers match 1965's level of 59.2%, according to Morgan Stanley.
- Housing prices have dipped 32% since they peaked in mid-2006, again for the 50th straight month realtors call a bottom to the decline.
- Weekly first time jobless claims continued their record setting levels above 400,000 for the 17th straight week.
- The average length of time to find a job has surged to a new record, 40.4 weeks.
- The labor force participation rate fell to a new low, 63.9% not seen since the early 1980s.
- Including those who quit looking but desire employment, the broader unemployment rate reached 16.1%.
- Gold topped historic numbers last week, closing above $1660/ounce.

I believe President Obama and Congress sealed their political fate last week and I am hopeful revolution will begin with the election of leaders, not self-serving politicians in 2012. A quick read of history will point to failed governments following the same path as the United States. We will not have societal Armageddon tomorrow, but our standard of living, and more importantly future generations' standard of living, will continue to decline.

Things You Don't Know (8/17/2011)

It's easy to watch the news and feel the economy is improving. Comically the performance of the Dow Jones is blasted at us each evening as the key indicator of economic success in America. It becomes more ironic when one thinks of Larry Kudlow shouting accolades of "Green Shoots" across the CNBC airwaves, but our neighbors are losing their jobs and homes. The Obama administration's economic success is measured by the Dow, unemployment, and inflation. The numbers are reported as better than during the recession of the 1980s and especially better than the Great Depression. However, this is far from the truth.

Every evening the swings in the Dow are blasted across the airwaves as the measure of success of our country. However, the Dow has changed so dramatically no one should pay any attention to these numbers. The Dow is an index of 30 companies, originally started in 1896. In 1896 there were twelve companies in the Dow and only one remains existence today, General Electric. Since 1896 the "components," or 30 companies composing the index, have changed 48 times. Thus, a more technology weighted or health services weighted Dow can look nothing like the Dow of bygone years. When one adds inflation, as the Dow is unadjusted, the numbers become completely meaningless.

The unemployment numbers are currently 9.1% and considered the holy grail of whether we are better off than the Great Depression. Most people don't realize the methods of calculating the unemployment rate have changed. The most significant change came in 1994 when those out of work for more than a year were eliminated from the numbers, essentially reducing the count by 5 million and in 2003 the statistical models were changed. Using old methods brings the current U-6 rate to 23%, in line with the numbers of the 1930's.

The consumer price index (CPI) is the measure of inflation and it too has changed. The market basket of goods is to measure pricing averages as this index impacts policy and more importantly government dole like Social Security and Medicaid. Alan Greenspan argued the historic methods were invalid because, for example, if the price of a steak increased then consumers would substitute with hamburger. A somewhat valid argument until one considers rent, heating oil, and gasoline where there are no substitutions. Changes were made by Carter, Reagan, and Clinton to ensure inflation was not "overstated." Housing is indexed to "rent equivalents" and energy has been eliminated.

In essence, we are not comparing apples and apples to look at today versus yesterday. "*There are three kinds of lies: lies, damned lies and statistics.*" – Author Unknown

All Lots $79,900 (10/5/2011)

Driving to Gainesville (GA) one morning last week I passed a partially developed neighborhood with an enormous sign advertising, "All Lots $79,900 – Financing Available." I laughed as I looked at the subdivision: empty lots next to "McMansions" displaying overgrown weeds, and electrical boxes and sewer pipes growing out of the ground like trees. The eyesore of the undeveloped properties is obvious and a developer's dream is awash in a failed economy.

During the boom I was always troubled by such subdivisions; worthless land with infrastructure added and lots sold like South Florida swampland. Exorbitant prices were supported by the banking Ponzi scheme. How come no one every asked why a piece of dirt was nearly $350,000 per acre I wondered? Farmland returns value and is the reason people homesteaded. However since the first post-WWII subdivisions in Levittown Americans have succumbed to a delusion of home ownership as a measure of success.

Imagery fuels this desire as Hollywood's settings range from Beverly Hills and Orange County to Chicago's North Lakeside Drive or beachfront on any shoreline. The middle class believes homes should be large and spacious when the affordable reality is quite opposite. Maybe the "Real Housewives..." should be set in a Toll Brothers or KB Homes three bedroom house in Orange County, Florida to generate a realistic picture of middle class life. In that show Mom and Dad would both work 50 hours per week and good times are replaced with conversations of budgets and staying afloat.

The media continues to find false hope week after week of real estate market bottoms or economic turnaround. Housing starts are the lowest in recorded history, and loans to purchase a home are unattainable. The biggest criminals have been exonerated by "too big to fail" and continue to profit, and taxpayers now hold one-third of foreclosed properties. Instead of reporting on "Obamavilles" and digital soup lines of 45 million food stamp recipients a National Association of Realtors monthly press release reporting "pricing bottom reached" is promoted as gospel to only be contradicted the following month.

The dreams remain alive for a life now gone; large houses, jet skis, and oversized trucks, but signs for $79,900 lots still fly. As businesses shutter, mayhem by youthful mobs continues, prices rise and wages stagnant I hope reality will set in. Across the country there are families living the dream in brand new, overpriced homes looking at the overgrown remnants of lost subdivisions and lost dreams. Someday soon the sign will promote the real value, "All Lots - Worthless."

7 NANNY STATE

The Wrong Debate (9/9/09)

Health Insurance is not a right. It is not an entitlement, not a guarantee. I have searched the Constitution for insight into the current debate and noted that the founding fathers did not identify health insurance as an inalienable right. Stop and note, I did not say that health care is not a right. What is taking place in America today is the wrong debate and it is packaged under words like "health care reform". But, no one is debating whether health care in America is adequate; in fact it is easily described as the best in the world with people seeking medical treatment in this country from around the world. The issue is cost, and who should pay for health care.

Unfortunately, when the wrong debate takes place too many people get trapped by the play on emotions. I always suggest taking a step back and asking "why"?

Why do we have health insurance? The health insurance debate began 100 years ago as medical technology improved and Progressives made calls for compulsory insurance. In 1920, these attempts failed as they were associated with the socialist policies of the Germans in WWI. By WWII though, more expensive hospital stays, successes by the "Blues", and tax incentives made employee benefit programs such as insurance appealing. Ordinary citizens put a priority on access to health care, regardless of cost. Prior to that time, we paid our doctor when we needed treatment. Of course, sometimes a person did not have the resources to pay their doctor, but that did not mean they would not receive treatment. Unlike today, it was treatment first and pay later.

Why does health care in America cost so much? First, medical malpractice has increased the cost of basic overhead requiring doctors and hospitals to charge fees to offset this cost. Second, the government will only pay certain amounts on Medicare claims thus requiring all other payers to subsidize the costs of benefits to these recipients.

Why do doctors get paid so much? One of my concerns is this new debate in America over wages, basically class envy. In short, if being a brain surgeon were easy then we all would be doing it. I watched the anesthesiologist insert an epidural in my wife's spine prior to the delivery of our son. I am a smart guy, an engineer that handled hazardous chemicals with explosive potential, but you could not pay me enough money to do what he did. These educated, skillful individuals deserve every amount of the wages they earn as they ho***ld our lives in their hands. I want absolutely the best person doing that job. I do not see a doctor's job as a "staff" position equivalent to a mid-level manager nor do I feel my plumber should earn more. Heck, Congressmen earn $176,000/year and doctors are more educated, more trained, and care about me.

I have not offered a solution, because now we can debate the issue. Let's agree that everyone is entitled to health care, but not to health insurance. Let's agree that we have a great medical system with the best doctors in the world. And, let's agree that health insurance is a nice convenience to offset catastrophe, but as individuals we are accountable for the health services we use and need to pay our bills. A large, government run health care insurance program is not the solution to the problems at hand

What is Government's Role? (9/30/2009)

Recently I engaged in an email discussion with a close friend regarding the health care debate. The more interesting aspect was the redirect from her attacking a position I had taken regarding privacy rights, unrelated to health care, to an attack stating that I did not think seniors deserved end of life counseling.

I have to be honest with you, before August I had never considered phrases like "death panels" or "end of life counseling". But, as we all know, these terms hit the airwaves and became dinner talk for many of us. I personally felt Sarah Palin did a great service to everyone by bringing attention to just one of the many possible issues open for debate within healthcare reform legislation. At the same time though, Ms. Palin's methodology of exaggeration damages her credibility and makes it tougher to engage in genuine conversation regarding a sensitive issue.

After several readings of my email reply to my friend I could not find anywhere I said seniors did not deserve end of life counseling. Carefully I crafted a reply to my friend, one that I want to share with you:

"First, I never said seniors should not have end of life counseling, how could you infer that from my note? But, let's presume they should. The first question to answer would be who should provide it? I certainly would not want a government staff employee to provide this service. What would we base their performance appraisal on, the number of seniors that refuse future health care benefits or the number of seniors they counsel that argue they want to live longer? Furthermore, if the government is going to provide end of life counseling, shouldn't there be benefits for marriage counseling, divorce counseling, parenting counseling and middle-age counseling to ensure you are on the right track? It is obvious any hazardous activity would have to be counseled."

I do not think the founding fathers intended for the State to provide this level of counseling or care to its citizens. In 1776 I believe the focus of the founding fathers was on the concepts of liberty and freedom due to the recent tyranny and oppression which they had just escaped and shed blood to have independence. The founding fathers stood firm and fought for our freedoms. Unfortunately, I believe time has caused descendants of these men to forget why we are the best country on earth and why other countries want to be like us.

We must look at history to get perspective and context. The founding fathers wanted a limited government because they knew what happened when a dependency (junkie/dealer) relationship is created. Over time other statesmen have endeavored to remind us how to avoid becoming a victim of our own success and desires. Gerald Ford said it succinctly, "A government big enough to give you everything you want is a government big enough to take from you everything you have."

I do not believe government health care reform should involve end of life counseling. My belief is not due to lack of sympathy or compassion, but because I believe it is not the role of the State to provide, fund, or facilitate that counseling. The role of government my friend is what we should debate.

No Insurance Mandate (10/7/2009)

As the debate regarding health care insurance rages around me I have found myself frustrated by comments and concerns made by friends and family and the threat of insurance mandates. Currently, I have no health insurance. Arguably, this may not be the best decision in my case, but it is my current situation. I understand I am now "self-insured" and if something happens I have to pay for it.

Crazily, I have friends and family who cannot imagine a life without health insurance. The government is also contemplating an insurance mandate; if you fail to buy insurance you will be fined. Since the IRS is the enforcer of this, I see it as a tax increase, especially considering the amount is approximately $3,800/year. What really bothers me is the idea of an insurance mandate when insurance, by definition, is coverage by contract in which one party agrees to indemnify or reimburse another for loss that occurs under the terms of the contract. Mandating a contract erodes the market forces that should lower prices.

This summer I was vacationing with my family and found myself in need of emergency care. I mentally debated for several hours my options: do not seek care, self-medicate, visit an urgent care, or head to the ER. Ultimately I spent seven hours in the emergency room, received outstanding service and a plethora of intravenous medicines. The doctors clearly discussed with me options of spending the night, further analysis, and how to proceed. Market forces were at work – no unnecessary tests were made, and I full participated in the decision making process. Upon returning from vacation the bill was waiting in the mailbox. At first glance the amount concerned me, but I quickly analyzed the numbers and realized the amount due was equal to two months of former family health care premiums. Since I had not made premium payments in prior five months I knew I was better off., and more than likely, I will not have any significant events before the end of the year.

I was disgusted when one family member recommended we not pay the bill. She said that she just ignores them and the hospital will ultimately write it off as indigent or uncollectable. Of course, they will just have to pass these costs onto others. Another friend was appalled that we do not have insurance and wondered what we would do if we had to go to the doctor. I made the economic argument above, it is cheaper to have high deductible insurance and pay as you go, but it fell on deaf ears. Of course, she depends on doctors for everything, has significant monthly prescription requirements, and does not have savings of her own to pay.

People make life choices and I believe too many consumers choose to live for the moment: buying a boat, car, cable television, or even a cellular phone. Losing material possessions due to an illness is sad, but not catastrophic, it's just stuff. Failing to take personal responsibility should not result in mandated insurance programs and erosion of personal freedoms. My reforms and solutions are much simpler: require people to pay for the services they use and hold them accountable, and yes they may go broke in the process, reign in the cost of malpractice through tort reform, and modify regulations to allow interstate purchase of insurance thus equalizing premiums across the states. No one will be denied quality health care and the market will adjust prices appropriately.

Cruise Ships (10/21/2009)

One of the highlights of a cruise ship trip to the Bahamas is a visit to the local market. Some bargaining will take place; you will feel good about your purchase, getting a great price, and the vendor will have sold one of his wares. This system works and has stood the test of time because there are no price floors or ceilings.

For example if I want to buy a handmade blanket for $20 in the above example with a little negotiating I can buy the blanket for $16. Still not comfortable with the price, I can walk away and the vendor will make a finally offer of $14. Because I know there are three other vendors selling similar, not necessarily the same, blankets nearby I can refuse the offer. Both of us are free to negotiate, up or down, in this scenario. I can pay $14, the vendor can lower his price to $13, or the deal can come to an end.

What would happen if the cruise ship company decided to check each vendor to ensure they were worthy, provide them perks, and guarantee a certain number of customers each day or pay him for any lost business? Furthermore, the cruise ship company agrees they will take $5 from each vendor to guarantee these benefits. In this case, the vendor will be reluctant to freely negotiate; he knows there are additional costs involved in the transaction. And, he also knows the cruise ship will pay him for any lost customers. Suddenly, his willingness to negotiate has been eroded by the establishment of a floor (guaranteed minimum) of business by the cruise ship company.

We can further complicate this scenario by supposing the cruise ship company requires the vendor to charge no more than$15 per blanket for anyone over 62 years old. Of course, people over 62 have much more free time and travel much more because they are large consumers of the cruise ship company's services and this perk helps the company attract more clients. However, the unintended consequence of this idea is the vendor loses revenue because his costs have not changed but yet he cannot charge more than $15 per blanket to those over 62. Thus, when I approach him, at age 42, his willingness to negotiate with me has been eroded further and I am forced to pay $20 or $21 for the blanket. Throughout the bazaar this is the case because all of the vendors are forced by the cruise ship company to charge less for blankets to older people, and pay the $5 fee (tax) for benefits and perks.

Free markets will work without a problem when left alone as they have for thousands of years. Buyers will always get the lowest price and sellers will maximize profits. Unfortunately, intervention by a single entity can have huge impacts within the market. The same is true in the current health care insurance debate or any other part of our economy where the government injects monies. Anytime this happens one group of individuals will benefit while the rest of the population pays more and subsidizes false market forces. The most recent example was the catastrophic failure and unintended consequences of "cash for clunkers". As reported, dealers did not come down on prices because the consumer was subsidized by tax payers to take home a car, not to negotiate. Ironically, the biggest beneficiary of this program was foreign labeled dealers, thus monies were artificially transferred via the program to foreign corporations that benefited from the spike in sales.

Merry Christmas from Congress (12/23/2009)

As the Christmas holiday comes upon us this week I feel compelled to take a look at our government and what has happened in the past year. Driving this is speculation over whether Senator Harry Reid will force a vote on healthcare Christmas Eve. Personally, I hope the vote is squashed, not because of my feelings on government run health care, but because of the actions and methods of this new Democratic Party run government.

I am concerned by the cloak of secrecy and selling votes to force healthcare to fruition. In contrast to Congress' actions right now, I have had the opportunity to sit on several government boards in Florida and the "Sunshine Laws" have been drilled into me. On one hand they are frustrating as these laws regarding open, transparent government make it difficult to negotiate contracts, bid on projects, and protect the tax payer in some instances. But, this smaller issue is far outweighed by eliminating secrecy in government. Florida is renowned for putting a high priority on the public's right of access to governmental meetings and records. In fact, the principles of open government are not only embodied in Florida statutes, but also are guaranteed in the state Constitution.

Similar to the Sunshine Laws, President Obama proposed "Sunlight Before Signing" stating "Too often bills are rushed through Congress and to the president before the public has the opportunity to review them. As president, I will not sign any non-emergency bill without giving the American public an opportunity to review and comment on the White House website for five days." However, this has been done far less than 50% of the time since taking office. Additionally, House Speaker Nancy Pelosi famously declared on September 24th she would make the healthcare bills available for review at least 72-hours prior to any votes, but as we know that was not the case. The American people learned how this new majority party government would work when the stimulus bill passed last spring was voted on without accommodation for members of Congress to read it, rushed through for signature, and even President Obama did not follow his own directive for "Sunlight Before Signing".

Open government protects us, the citizens from potential tyranny by our elected officials. I am dismayed at closed-door meetings in Washington, the President calling members of a single party to the Whitehouse, or caucus meetings to promise hundreds of millions of dollars to a single congressional district or state. Sadly, at the national level straw polls are taken, potential votes counted, and strategies are determined to allow some members of congress to even vote "Nay" in an effort to protect them from political backlash over certain legislation. Thus, a bill may pass by the slimmest majority, but a majority nonetheless when a single party controls Congress; all in sharp contrast to Florida's open government laws.

This week much political maneuvering regarding procedures will take place while most of us are distracted with holiday events. One must wonder why if the proposed healthcare bill is critical to one-sixth of our economy, our well-being, and best for the country then why must negotiation be done secretly. Like Santa Claus, the Senate will come together Christmas Eve to deliver the "gift" of healthcare over the objection of the majority of Americans.

Race Horses and Jackasses (4/14/2010)

A race horse is a beautiful animal, treated with care and coveted by its owner and caretaker. In return for all of the positive attention this animal will run hard and fast, win races, and in some cases bring home millions of dollars in winnings. By contrast, a jackass is not as beautiful, he's stubborn, and typically abused to get work done. My friend Barry once shared with me a saying his attorney told him about divorce court, "ex-wives should treat their ex-husbands like race horses and they will bring home the winnings. Instead, too many ex-wives take them for granted, don't appreciate them, and make their lives hard, treating them like jackasses so they act like jackasses." In my opinion, any relationship could be described the same way: employer and employee, husband and wife, parents and teenager. I would also say the same holds true in politics and the current members of Congress seem to have started treating constituents like mules to do work. Ironically it seems to be the party that uses a donkey to represent itself that has taken this approach.

I must offer, the poster child for audacity and egotism in the Democrat party is local Congressman Alan Grayson. Orlando television station WFTV reported his outburst at a Perkins Family restaurant where a small group of his republican constituents were meeting. There are two sides to every story, but Grayson continues to build a reputation built on insults, outlandish statements, and ignorance of his constituents. In the video he states he knows exactly what his constituents are worth when he says, "There are 308 million people that pay my salary ($174,000/yr). Do you know what that breaks down to per person?" A little quick math shows Grayson knows it is $0.0006 per person. To me, it sounds like Grayson considers his constituents valueless mules, not successful race horses.

The Democrats faced supposed name calling and threats as a result of passing healthcare. In the aftermath of disregarding the legislative process for the sake of unilaterally passing an agenda disliked by the majority of American people they have reacted with surprise to the dislike for their actions, both as a party and personally. But, hell bent on passage they treated the American people with disrespect and total disregard. Thus, not listening and treating constituents like jackasses instead of race horses that bring home winnings has come back to haunt them. In the days after healthcare passage the media reported how horrible treatment had been including threats and racial slurs against Congressmen. With thousands of people on hand, from both sides, that afternoon it is amazing not a single video or recording has been forthcoming offering proof.

From the Republican side the best example of failing to treat others like race horses would come down to the floor debates regarding healthcare. At the same time though, no personal attacks were made in that venue, but there are those on the blogging and reporting side that offered up more questionable statements.

As children we are all taught the Golden Rule. However, researching this column and having watched the recent political process I would assert the disregard for the constituency comes not from personal hatred but understanding how little we are valued when compared to the lobbyists offering millions of dollars. Even if every citizen of Volusia County pulled together against our own Congresswoman Kosmas, by Congressman Grayson's math the influence on her would only be about $300. I guess Grayson, Kosmas, and every other Congressman can afford to treat constituents like jackasses.

8 JUDICIARY

Cable, Cellular, and Lawyers (11/11/2009)

It is amazing how certain industries seem to survive, regardless of the quality of service they deliver. As a consumer I am pretty easy going, but I do believe in accountability. Basically, I am just old-fashioned, deliver on your word and do what you promise. There are three industries though where this does not to be the case: cable television, cellular telephones, and law.

My experiences with cable and cellular companies began about 20 years ago. This is when I discovered the cable company could promise you an installation arrival time, but that was unrelated to the reality of when they might arrive. Throughout the last 25 years I have planned a day around "getting cable" and found myself at the mercy of the cable company regarding my time. If promised 9:00 am -noon, I have patiently waited and realized at 1:15p no one was coming. What do I do next? Leave? Call? And of course, once cable is installed if it fails or you need upgraded services one will be trapped in automated voice mail systems, in long lines at their offices, or without television.

Cellular telephones were supposed to make my life easier. I bought my first phone in 1988, a Panasonic Transportable, about the size of a dictionary and weighing a couple of pounds. The idea was I would not have to stop at a pay phone to call ahead, reschedule, or stay in touch with my family. As much as it was a novelty at that time, with my $1.50/minute charges, it was a business tool to serve the purpose of making phone calls. However, the phone dropped calls. Every two to three years for the last 20 years I have bought a new phone, always hoping that the latest model would not drop a call. But, the same problems continue today, dropped calls and lousy connections. I learned and never make critical calls on a cellular phone while moving. I have paid thousands of dollars to various companies, after considering all of the mergers, and yet the most basic service piece, making a call, has not been satisfactorily delivered.

Furthermore, the cellular companies have continued to miss the mark as buying a phone is not about telephone service, but cameras, MP3 players, and texting. I just want to make a call. At the same time each of us is personally robbed every day we use our phone. We are forced to listen to voice mail system prompts that run up our charges. The next time you make a call to a cellular phone, pay attention to how long it takes to wait for the voice mail announcement to complete and leave a message. Or, call your voice mail to retrieve messages. Why can't I skip the message? After years I know the routine and what to do. But, I am convinced this system is designed to collect a few minutes more from each of us, resulting in millions of profits for the cellular companies.

Attorneys are often the target of jokes and attacks. Most likely this stems from the perception of the lack of quality in the service they deliver. Unlike any other industry I know, this is a professional industry where a non-refundable payment is required before service is rendered. Regardless of the quality of service delivered, your non-refundable retainer has been captured. You have no mechanism to question the quality of service or the process that was used. I am convinced that attorney's know they deliver the shoddiest services because of this payment process.

Are these rants? I don't think so. Instead, I believe we are all entitled to a respectful relationship with the vendors and service providers whom we engage. However, when monopolies begin to exist, there is no competition, or there is no process for client satisfaction the quality of service degrades rapidly.

Monitoring the Judiciary (11/25/2009)

Government in the United States creates three distinct branches: Legislative, Executive, and Judicial. The Legislative and Executive branches are scrutinized, questioned, and monitored for performance daily. In November of each year we return to the polls to keep incumbents or vote them out of office; an easy decision to make based on their public actions in office. I argue we do not hold our judicial branch to the same level of accountability, but yet the decisions made by judges have more irreparable individual and societal impact than the other two branches of government.

In many states, judges are appointed to the bench by elected political leaders. This is true for example of the Supreme Court. When a Supreme Court vacancy comes about the media scrutinizes a President's appointment as the Supreme Court Justice will sit for life and have much influence over the future of the country. Significant cases such as *Roe v. Wade* and *Miranda* are familiar to all of us. At the same time, lesser known cases such as *Kelo v. City of New London* can impact any private property owner.

At the state and county level the method of putting a judge on the bench may either be by appointment or vote. Although preferred, voting brings risks as many voters lack education about judicial candidates, and another conflict is created because who wants to see a judge campaigning for election? I can just imagine a platform like, "I'll let you off every time if you elect me!" More important than election though is an adequate recall or confirmation process. In Volusia County this exists, but there is a bigger problem; we have no way to gauge the performance of the judiciary.

In sharp contrast to the local judicial branch, the legislative and executive branches of government are easy to monitor as voting on legislation is tracked, collated, and reported. When judges make bad decisions the only course of action is a complaint to the Judicial Qualifications Commission (JCQ) or filing an Appeal. The JCQ is a one-sided process allowing little opportunity for fairness to the complainant, and the appellate process is quite expensive. Recent Supreme Court appointee Justice Sotomayor is an excellent example of the failure of a proper judicial monitoring process. In her case Appeals were filed and her rulings were overturned 60% of the time. She may be a nice woman with sensitivities to certain groups, but her abuse of judicial discretion cost those who had to appeal to overturn her failed rulings. In other words, good people had to spend time and money to recover what was correct but had to argue against her errors in her position. An average person making bad decisions more than 5-10% of the time would be fired from their job, she averaged 60%.

I propose the establishment of a monitoring system to educate the public regarding judicial rulings and trends. I have heard speculation from friends about judges that tend to favor one group over another regardless of circumstances. An example of monitoring would be a Family Court system to track rulings by judge and by parent. The same could be done regarding fines in traffic court, sentencing by race and sex in criminal court, and whether favoritism is given to corporations or individuals in civil court.

Many of us believe justice is blind and pride ourselves in the belief judicial prejudice does not exist in the judiciary as we believe it does in other countries. However, with no quantifiable monitoring system I argue good people and families are harmed irreparably by the unaccountable Judiciary every day.

The View (8/4/2010)

It is amazing how two people can look at the same consideration and see two distinct things. Even a single feature can look different depending on the direction from which it is approached. I live next to a 3,200 foot mountain peak, Mt. Yonah, and admire its beauty every time I drive home. If I approach Mt. Yonah from the Northwest I see a gently rising tree covered mountain, rising majestically to the sky. However, approaching from the Southeast, to go home, the same mountain rises ominously with nearly vertical granite faces, stripped of any foliage and impossible to climb. Although this same peak is visible from miles around, the view and approach would change your perspective about climbing to the summit.

Politics, societal problems, and even relationships anecdotally reflect my mountain. Depending on the point of view taken to attack issues, problems can appear gradually solvable or insurmountable. For example, the oil spill in the Gulf can be viewed as an environmental tragedy or an engineering challenge. Chelsea Clinton's wedding last weekend was hyped as the wedding of the century, but to the residents of Rhinebeck, New York it was a media frenzy and security nightmare. What has been lost in American debate today is the understanding that debate accommodates differing views; one is not necessarily right or wrong. I learned several years ago feelings cannot be argued, only facts. However, if you watch the news closely, and monitor political debate, arguments center on emotions, feelings, and perceptions, not facts.

Last week a federal judge issued an injunction against Arizona's controversial immigration bill. This is a hot-button issue with differing views on how to solve a problem. I would argue what is missing is the discussion of the issue at hand. For example, Obama promised immigration reform, but after 19 months in office nothing has transpired leaving Arizona to deal with the issue and thus pushing a bill designed to move the issue to the spotlight. Armed with what I know, I could not possibly consider living in a border state due to the violence, costs, and breakdown in social order. However, I believe we should embrace people risking their lives to come to our country. What matters now is how we view the problem and work together to solve it; effective debate starts with understanding the view.

Tort Reform (1/5/2011)

A discussion about nationalized healthcare cannot take place without mentioning tort reform. In essence the thought is reducing litigation or damages will reduce costs to healthcare. Of course we could assume that would translate to all industries. Everyone remembers the lawsuit against McDonalds for serving hot coffee, spilled by the consumer, and McDonalds ultimately paying hundreds of millions of dollars. Similarly, businesses face threats of lawsuits daily from falls in parking lots or stores, misuse of products, or frivolous acts. A rampant industry of "legal theft" has been created by the television and billboard lawyers fishing for clients who may have an ailment never before considered, but with marketing and awareness suddenly thousands can suffer from imaginary problems, become part of a class lawsuit, and make money. The real winner is the law firm making millions in fees and taking a significant portion of the award.

Movies like *Erin Brokovich* and the many John Grisham films have reminded us of the sympathetic need for our ability to litigate. In these blockbuster films the destitute win against the big, bad corporation and remind us they are evil and must be punished. In other parts of the world citizens cannot sue for millions and must bear the cost of legal fees when initiating a lawsuit and the defendants costs should the lose. Neither method is perfect and create unintended consequences. Americans appear frivolous and greedy in seeking justice and other countries appear to favor the big company over the individual.

Unfortunately we all face other consequences of our system. Imagine driving your car down Flagler Avenue and having a bicycle run into you. Several weeks later you may find a television lawyer serving you with a lawsuit. Regardless of fault, your insurance company will pay, not even argue the case, as the TV lawyer pimp pursues an endless income stream from legal extortion. Similarly, a professional license is jeopardized by frivolous complaints and legal fees to defend proper decisions can cost tens of thousands. Imagine the numbers professionals in the financial industry accused of "losing money" during the collapse of 2008-2009. Of course, the likes of Bernie Madoff permanently tarnished the reputation of those exercising due diligence.

Regardless of fault, a system of arbitration to bypass the expense of discovery should be established, especially on an individual basis. Principles costs money and often settlement to find personal peace through dismissal is a better option, but a feeling of admission of guilt is created when no guilt is present. *"I do not add 'within the limits of the law' because law is often but the tyrant's will, and always so when it violates the rights of the individual."* – Thomas Jefferson

Changeling (8/24/2011)

My family and I recently watched the moving "Changeling" with Angelina Jolie. The movie itself was entertaining and focused on the efforts of a 1920's woman to recover her missing son. The issue at hand was the corruption of the Los Angeles Police Department after receiving bad press and their attempts to cover up shoddy police work. As we watched I found myself angered over the blatant misuse of authority. For example, when Jolie's character challenged the police department they had her committed to an LA psychological hospital; a warrantless incarceration without trial. Once behind the walls of the hospital it was nearly impossible for her to plead her case.

Watching the movie caused me to challenge my kids to compare the situation to events of today and instantly they commented on perception of law enforcement corruption and intimidation. Of course, the most obvious example is TSA's violation of the 4th Amendment at airport security check points and intimidation of people like Aaron Toney who was detained for 90 minutes, without arrest, by TSA on December 31 at Richmond, Virginia's airport when he removed his shirt and displayed the 4th Amendment on his chest.

In Philadelphia gun owner Mark Fiornio was nearly shot, detained and harassed for lawfully openly carrying a gun. A new FBI Advisory circular, "Communities Against Terrorism: Potential Indicators of Terrorist Activities Related to Military Surplus Stores" advises store owners to keep records of customers making lawful purchases but fitting a profile of self-preparedness.

In London two weeks ago government officials required Amazon.com to stop selling self-defense weapons while authorities simultaneously allowed riots to "run their course." Thus, the citizens lost the right to protect themselves in their own homes. Similarly, San Francisco authorities shut down cell-towers within the Bart system to prevent a possible riot from developing, but also leaving law abiding citizens with no mechanism for protection.

Regardless of examples I provide I must wonder when intimidation will stop and the rule of law will prevail. The movie "Changeling" highlighted corruption I could not believe existed. Ultimately, the 1930's Courts found in favor of their "own", but yet the corruption was known and documented. Like the Gestapo, TSA, police departments, and the National Guard will be asked to turn on citizens instead of protecting those, they are here "To Serve and Protect."

Lawyers (8/31/2011)

The problem in America with health care costs, insurance and even consumer costs is lawyers. I fly airplanes and recently was reading a placard in the aircraft, finding it idiotic because it states the obvious: "...failure to properly latch seat and heed all instructions can result in bodily injury or death." That placard is there due to a widow successfully suing Cessna when he adjusted his seat while climbing out on take-off. The incident was certainly not Cessna's fault but a jury ruled otherwise.

Some adventure sports like white water rafting and parachuting require a waiver before participating; again to head off lawsuits. Every amusement park in America has a warning to pregnant women and back pain sufferers at the front of each line to mitigate law suits. Similarly, my wife is pregnant and we were required to sign an 8-page disclaimer releasing the doctor of liability if the baby is harmed during birth due to law suits.

Recently I was in Mexico with my kids and took them to an attraction consisting of natural park area, snorkeling, tubing, and other experiences. Walking through the park there were no hand rails to protect against a fall, there were no cameras watching our every move, and there were no warning signs at each ride In fact, it was probably the nicest, cleanest, most cost-effective, freest park experience I have ever head; it existed without the oversight of lawyers fueling idiocracy.

Three weeks ago I traveled to Gulf Shores, Alabama and saw shocking "ambulance chaser" billboards. The law firms advertising were seeking clients who cleaned up the oil spill and "might" be exhibiting "any" symptoms of illness. Talk about fishing for monies and setting up for a class action lawsuit.

It is nearly impossible to turn on the evening news in Orlando, Florida without the advertising of a particular law firm shopping for clients to call regarding the latest disease, tragedy, or injury. The only justification for the persistent advertising is the successful income stream generated by settlements made just under the radar of large companies. These under $20,000 lawsuits filed frivolously but settled readily by insurance companies cut costs instead of risking larger expenses in court, a steady windfall for law firms.

Examples abound but now I must ask, is this the lawyers' fault or the juries making it easy to win "life's lottery" with a lawsuit. I don't know that caps on lawsuits are the right answer but I would assert less monies to attorneys and more to victims would make lawyers less likely to shop for victims and more likely to pursue justice.

9 MEDIA

Mainstream Media (9/23/2009)

When I was a kid there were three commercial televisions networks, PBS, and an independent station or two. News came from a 30-minute local broadcast at 6:00pm and was followed immediately by a 30-minute network newscast. The daily paper was on our driveway every morning and was supplemented by "The Today Show". Throughout the day AM radio would air news on the hour. That is the media with which I grew up, and not until Ted Turner's Cable News Network did the idea of 24-hour news flowing into our living room become a possibility. This was quickly followed by the abbreviated version with "Headline News". Ultimately, other entrepreneurs followed with "The Weather Channel", "C-Span", and areas of specific interest like financial news.

All of the above media suffer from their own problems, usually attributed to their delivery method. The 24-hour channels find themselves without enough information to fill the day so they turn to commentary. The daily newspaper is typically 24-48 hours behind events due to publishing and delivery methods. Lastly, the major networks conceive their stories in the morning and build a broadcast around a concept that is not reactive to change or daytime events.

Personally, I feel "news" means the presentation of information or events. Unfortunately, what many view as news is colored commentary or persuasive opinion. For example, "A man robbed a bank" would be objective news reporting. On the other hand, "A burly man from the low-income neighborhood robbed a bank" could paint an entirely different picture in your mind. The simple use of adjectives and commentary has flowed into the news and tainted the objectivity of reporting and the average person is historically ignorant to this manipulation by accepting formerly credible news outlets at face value.

I would assert all media is "mainstream." With television, newspaper, radio, and the internet we can access any news source at anytime. Every day I read multiple international and domestic newspapers, wire services, watch network news broadcasts, and scour several newsfeeds. I see trends in news and who is, or is not, reporting events. At the same time I also filter the adjectives and objectively form my own opinions. The insinuation of a domestic conspiracy in reporting is obvious when reviewing live, objective newsfeeds from around the world. I am intrigued by the three major networks presenting the same stories, in the same order day after day. I also wonder how major papers like the "New York Times" and "Washington Post" can have nearly identical front pages and editorial comments.

I believe the "Legacy" media is failing to provide objective reporting to its audience. Worse, it is not necessarily what, or how, it is reported, but the failure to report. For example, the "New York Times" made a conscious decision to withhold a story during the presidential election of 2008 that most likely would have changed the outcome of candidate choices. Most recently, the legacy broadcasting networks, the "New York Times", and the "Washington Post" failed to provide timely reporting of events leading up to the resignation of a government official. Once upon a time I believe these legacy information outlets prided themselves on getting "the scoop" but it appears that is no longer the case.

The term "Mainstream Media" implies an accusation or conspiracy to promote an agenda. Some object to this, but the pattern has emerged over decades. The new method of story absence, however, is a covert method to undermine the "mainstream" argument. Objectivity would allow me to form opinions and omission of news is more manipulative than colored commentary..

10 DOES ANYONE KNOW

Sheep (2/10/2010)

This past weekend was the Superbowl, a time honored tradition of getting together with friends, watching the game, cheering for fantastic football plays and watching commercials at halftime. I scoff at this as a continued hilarious process of entertaining the sheep, or the "sheeple" if you prefer. Sadly, I assert more people know the names of the quarterbacks of each team and not the names of their two Senators. Most people will know which team won the game, but cannot name which party has a majority in Congress. Lastly, the commercials will be recounted with detailed attention, but the average person cannot describe the details of the largest federal budget passed in history this last week.

I find myself an outcast because I don't watch the Superbowl, or follow professional football obsessively. I admit I don't follow any professional sports religiously, although I may know names, teams, or who leads a league at times. And of course, if I were invited to a game or race, I would joyfully attend. Preparing this week's column I had realized I had no idea who was playing, and did not care. I realized a long time ago I had no interest in watching millionaires who made no contribution to society run around on a field or court. When the players make the news it is usually due to beating their wife or girlfriend, an affair, drugs, or shooting. But yet, our society idolizes these players that have near superhuman strength.

With President Obama's populist push against the CEOs and executives of major corporations I must wonder why sports and Hollywood celebrities are exempt. The American people readily hand their money over to large entertainment corporations that provide obscene riches to a very few in an environment where nepotism is more likely to drive success than any type of skill. On the other hand, a successful businessman who risked his home, personal family life, and employed others is now demonized if he rises to a successful level. No one questioned the use of private aircraft and limousines by Paris Hilton, but the automotive executives that employ hundreds of thousands and whose company's stock is owned by the masses were chastised by Congress for wisely using their time to travel via an efficient means. Ironically, Nancy Pelosi travels every week via private aircraft from Washington, D.C. to California at taxpayer expense but that is not questioned.

President Obama has made it clear that to succeed in America by hard work, rising through the ranks, managing people, and running billion dollar corporations is bad. However, it is acceptable to sign a hundred million dollar contract to play games for a few years, and even get paid if hurt. Or, like Conan O'Brien to get $30 million to peacefully leave a contract at NBC. As much as his populist agenda is being promoted, it scares me to think about a lottery society where success is measured by luck rather than a society that favors hard work, risk, and rewards success. Life is not fair, everyone is not a winner, but America has led the world by everyone having the opportunity to succeed regardless of gender, race, or economics. The Romans distracted the people with entertainment, ran lotteries, and controlled the people to take taxes, and control the people. Governments know when the people are entertained they will turn their backs on the important issues and trust others to care for them, just like sheep. Sadly, it seems like the American people have become sheep who do not care. Now, I must ask, "Who won the game?"

Clintons equal Contradiction (5/5/2010)

When former Presidents speak their mind it is amazing how the media rushes to give credibility to their statements. I find it interesting that both former Bush's tend to keep their comments on the charitable and humanitarian side while both Carter and Clinton feel compelled to continue to govern and affect policy. Last week I wrote about former President Bush ("W") and what history may regard as the worst change to our civil liberties, enacting the Patriot Act. This week, Bill Clinton, and Hillary, must be called out for what they are, the greatest liars to ever hold the highest office in the United States.

Probably no quote in history can be described as more concerning than, "*I did not have sexual relations with that woman, Miss Lewinsky. I never told anybody to lie, not a single time; never. These allegations are false. And I need to go back to work for the American people. Thank you.*" With the audacity of a teenager, Bill Clinton looked directly into the cameras and lied to the American people. Quickly defended by supporters and leftists, Clinton was given a pass on this issue as his behavior was regarded as irrelevant to the presidency and his ability to govern. Much ado was subsequently made regarding his statements and it took seven months to finally come to an admission of "improper physical relationship" on August 17, 1998.

During his presidency Clinton dealt with two attacks on American soil, the first World Trade Center bombing and the Oklahoma City Bombing. Obviously Oklahoma City made an impact on Clinton because it drove him to recently make comments comparing Tim McVeigh to the Tea Partiers of today. On April 16, Clinton said that "legitimate" comparisons can be drawn between today's grass-roots anger and resentment toward the government and the right-wing extremism that bubbled up prior to the bombing of a federal building in Oklahoma City 15 years ago. Personally, I can find no comparison to Tim McVeigh, a militia movement sympathizer, who sought revenge against the federal government for "Waco" which had ended in the deaths of 76 people exactly two years earlier. In contrast, the Tea Party has gained coverage in the media with credibility as average citizens rightfully protesting, under the First Amendment, the new debt policies of the current administration.

The Clintons' contradiction seems to come from protesting against the actions of the government, when a Republican is in office, which is acceptable, versus when a Democrat is running the kingdom, unacceptable. Clinton ordered the Waco attack and Obama is fueling debt which will be put on the shoulders of generations of Americans to come, and both have generated protests. Clinton hated the Vietnam War and policies of Republican President Nixon, as quoted on June 9, 1969, the Frederick, Maryland *Post* ran an article by Tom Cullen on antiwar sentiment among the 29 American Rhodes Scholars attending Oxford. "And that's the way it should be," says William J. Clinton, 22, of Hot Springs, Ark., "There would be something wrong with us if we could put the war out of our minds when our friends are being shot up in Vietnam."

Hillary Clinton said it best though, in her 2003 tirade on the floor of the Senate, " I am sick and tired of people who say that if you debate and you disagree with this administration, somehow you're not patriotic, and we should stand up and say, "WE ARE AMERICANS AND WE HAVE A RIGHT TO DEBATE AND DISAGREE WITH ANY ADMINISTRATION!" Both Clintons want their right to protest, but not your right to protest against Democrats.

Blaming Others (7/21/2010)

Most weeks it is easy to write this column; I find a plethora of news and political stupidity that easily becomes fodder. Sometimes though, like this week, it becomes more difficult and I will ask for suggestions from friends. I was intrigued when my friend Bob suggested I write about the trend these days to blame others for our problems. In our short conversation I realized he was right, the whole idea of personal responsibility in America is gone. When I think about changes like this I always try to look back in time, through the eyes of my grandfather, to see how America has changed.

Examples abound regarding blaming others: Hurricane Katrina, Attention Deficit Disorder, Restless Leg Syndrome, liability litigation, Obama on Bush, and even the Toyota sudden acceleration. For example, one-hundred years ago if our children misbehaved they were disciplined, re-directed, and strong parenting was done; today we give them a pill. The same holds for new diseases, like Restless Leg Syndrome, heavily promoted by pharmaceutical companies and appearing weekly. The recent Toyota sudden acceleration claims were repudiated by the NTSB as driver error pushing the accelerator; I am sure the liability attorneys are profoundly disappointed.

Falling off a curb at a merchant, or falsely stepping in front of a car has grown into an entire industry. These attorneys do not go after millions, instead they seek a nominal amount, about $25k, from the defendants insurance company; just enough to make settling easier and better for the insurance company, but a cash cow for the law firms. Successful industries advertise; watch television or read billboards to see the proliferation of attorney's offering to "help". Hurricane Katrina was the ultimate blame game, as it appears the people of New Orleans had nothing to do with their decision to remain in the path of a Category 5 hurricane, and President Obama has continued that mantra by using the former President as his scapegoat at least ten times by my count in various speeches. My grandfather would have owned his failures and handled issues facing him, as I believe most people would have 100 years ago. Sadly, it is far easier to blame others, take a pill, and avoid personal responsibility. I wonder what our country will look like in another decade after blaming all of our problems on others.

King and Queen (8/11/2010)

Much ado was made last week regarding the Obama's and their lavish travels. Our presidents have historically found themselves in a conflictingly awkward position, servants to the taxpayers, but yet head of state. With the press covering trips to Spain and Chicago in the same week, there was discussion regarding the cost to taxpayers by the major news networks. The criticism was not only domestic, but extended to Western newspapers overseas. Ms. Obama's trip to Spain required a $140,000 in aircraft costs and nearly another $100,000 in security costs.

By comparison, many Americans found their life and opportunity worsening last week. Unemployment showed stagnant growth conditions, coming in twice as bad as predicted and including a downward revision for June. The USDA reported a record 40.8 million Americans received food stamps in June. My research showed in 2008 the number averaged 24.8 million, and a record 35 million were reported in September 2009. Three years have passed since the Great Recession started and trillions have been spent, but fundamentally America's economy has remained on the brink of failure. Remember the fat-finger stock trade? Have you tried to get a loan or re-finance? Look at the number of homes for sale all around and try finding a buyer. Among other recent reports was Social Security is now operating in the red, approximately 28% of mortgages are underwater, Fannie Mae had losses and is seeking bailouts, and consumers continue to withdraw from spending.

Conservative news outlets have jumped on the bandwagon of criticizing Ms. Obama for her trip, especially while many Americans are suffering. But, before jumping to conclusions, the first question is whether the Obama's travels are excessive compared to the last half dozen presidents. The Obama's are taking care of us, according to them; maybe these two people are deserving of grand vacations, at taxpayer expense. The people of the Gulf of Mexico would have benefitted from the publicity and international focus Spain is enjoying, just as Ms. Obama touted in June. If I were advising the Obama's I would suggest they learn humility, stop golfing and entertaining, quit campaigning, roll up their sleeves, and get to know America. The Obama's need to come to my neighborhood and meet real, hardworking, hurting Americans; parents working overtime unable to afford $20 for a meal out. However, royalty never visits peasants.

Together We Thrive? (1/19/2011)

We must remember Rahm Emanuel's words, "never let a good crisis go to waste" when examining our President's speech last week. It is amazing the office of the President, for purposes of offering condolences to the families of six murder victims and 14 injured, could exploit the opportunity to start the 2012 Presidential campaign. Can you imagine planning a speech for a country dealing with a heinous massacre and yet giving thought to producing 13,000 Tee-Shirts with the political slogan, "Together we Thrive"? I am concerned so many feel willing to give the political establishment a pass, in fact admire them for tactless, grotesque behavior so obviously filled with self promotion over those they govern. I remain steadfast in my opinion that leader's rise naturally by supporting and promoting their followers; not seeking the glory of the limelight or by utilizing and politicizing opportunities. What are the odds Congressman Giffords opened her eyes after President Obama's visit, leaving him to announce it to the country? The news was delivered like a Sunday morning preacher telling his flock what they want to hear and consumed without suspicion regarding this questionable coincidence.

Sadly, the politicization of Tucson was unavoidable, and I am too young to make comparisons to similar assassination attempts like Reagan, Ford, Wallace, King, Kennedy, Malcolm X, Truman, Long, Roosevelt F., Roosevelt T., McKinley, or Garfield. The reporting of such events prior to Kennedy was primarily via radio and newspaper, and Kennedy's assassination brought us the immortalized words of Walter Cronkite, but without opinion and speculation. The common theme in all of these attacks trends as a mentally deranged individual acting independently, seeking attention and lashing out at society. Last week, there was no need for the President's call to examine the discourse of self-governance, or to repeatedly mention a need to prompt reflection and debate. In short, a single, mentally ill man, Jared Lee Loughner killed six people and the wheels of justice will run him over and serve the appropriate sentence. In the meantime, the reporters and trusted news pundits should be held accountable for inaccurate reporting and we should be disgusted by the President's abuse of a sad event. We the people should encourage our elected officials to steer clear of the politics and calls for limits on free speech and restrictions on guns; instead understanding there are sick individuals among our 300 million and the actions of one do not represent groups, beliefs, or politics.

Nuclear Meltdown (5/25/2011)

This past week I counted at least four meltdowns, all covered with vigor, in the media headlines. Probably the most obscure and curious regarding the hype to most Americans was the arrest, indictment, and release of IMF Chief Dominique Strauss-Kahn. Little do many of my countrymen understand regarding monetary policy, let alone the calls for an end to the dollar as the reserve currency by Strauss-Kahn. The second meltdown was the failure of the Gingrich campaign to gain traction. Laughably, the most academic of a possible Republican field of presidential nominees, fell flat before starting. Like Strauss-Kahn, Newt melted down.

Meltdown number three was President Obama extinguishing his fiery return in the polls by crossing middle-east ally Israel with a call to return to territory held 44 years ago. The contradictory nature of Obama is puzzling as a blind-eye is turned toward our own border issues and we idly watch killing of refugees seeking democracy in Syria. But, the President is pro-Hamas supporting the terrorist organization publicly as far back as May 2008. Israel's Prime Minister Netanyahu skillfully schooled our President on the fallacies of his position and Obama's action may be the beginning of his re-election meltdown. Finally, the mainstream pundits could not get enough of the Terminator's marriage meltdown, number four last week, as revelations exposed infidelity and a love child with a household staff member. Each of these personal meltdowns, in my opinion, is rooted in ego and self-interest.

Sadly though, the most important nuclear meltdown in the world is not garnering any media coverage and is similarly rooted in ego and self-interest. However, this meltdown over the next 30 years will result in many unnecessary deaths and cancers worldwide. On March 11, 2011 the historic earthquake rocked northern Japan, suspiciously damaging nuclear reactors, but denied by Japanese government. A newly released TEPCO report this week contains a disaster timeline stating within 5 hours of the quake fuel rods were exposed and rapidly melting, and within 16 hours Reactor No. 1's rods had melted down and dropped to the bottom of the reactor. Similar events occurred in Reactors 2 and 3. Today the reactors are continuing to spew radiation and radioactive water is flowing to groundwater and the ocean. Worse than Chernobyl, Fukushima has become the world's first nuclear meltdown. Curiously, the four men in personal meltdowns garner far more coverage, but every plant, animal, and human being in the Northern hemisphere is now poisoned by the ineptness of a government and power company that chose to hide their failures to protect their egos.

Little Noticed News (6/1/2011)

Oprah, Republican presidential candidate implosions, and Obama's Irish roots seem to dominate the news. On a national and international level none of these newsworthy events will impact most Americans. Instead, I argue there is an entire underlying level of news taking place nationwide, some of which gets a brief mention on one of the cable or broadcast networks, but most of the news disappears not to be heard from again. America is changing, and changing rapidly. Willfully civil rights and constitutional guarantees are being eroded, and yet a blind eye is turned. Below I have listed examples from the last three weeks.

On May 22, 2011 - a Santa Fe, NM high school announced TSA would pat-down students as part of security to enter Prom. From TSA's own web site, the agency's mission is, "The Transportation Security Administration protects the Nation's transportation systems to ensure freedom of movement for people and commerce." Nowhere is a high school or sports event mentioned, and I cannot imagine being groped on my last night in high school.

May 21, 2011 – Mark Fiornio strolled through downtown Philadelphia lawfully, openly, carrying his permitted gun. The issue at hand is Mr. Fiornio was detained, nearly shot, and charges brought against him for disorderly conduct and reckless endangerment. He tried to explain to police offers he had a permit and cited the statutory laws allowing him to open carry. Local authorities are warning gun owners that they will be "inconvenienced" if they carry unconcealed handguns in the city.

May 15, 2011 – The Indiana Supreme Court, 3-2, ruled people have no right to resist officers who enter their homes under the premise it is in the greater public good and would minimize confrontation. Additionally, the Indiana Court ruled police do not need to knock to serve a search warrant.

May 17, 2011 – Historically police offers required probable cause and a search warrant before breaking into a home. That changed with the Supreme Court's ruling in Kentucky v. King.

Ruling 8-1 the justices gave police more leeway to break into homes or apartments in search of illegal drugs when they suspect the evidence otherwise might be destroyed. Justice Ruth Bader Ginsburg dissented, fearing the ruling gave police an easy way to ignore 4th Amendment protections against unreasonable searches and seizures.

In each of the above cases I can easily see the argument for "greater good", "public safety" and other pansy excuses. Sadly, "we the people" are continuing to allow our freedoms to incrementally erode away. In one week, four cases that have far reaching circumstances. As a reminder, blood was shed for The Fourth Amendment, which assures that "the right of the people to be secure in their persons, houses, papers, and effects, against unreasonable searches and seizures, shall not be violated,"

The Media Elects Presidents (6/8/2011)

Over the last 50 years I believe there has been a dramatic turn in Presidential elections. Arguably the headline, "Dewey Defeats Truman" in 1948 is reflective of media bias and anticipation toward election outcomes. Most academics will acknowledge the 1960 Presidential debate outcome was not determined by the quality of the candidate speeches, but instead by appearance on television. Nixon articulated much stronger responses but was no match for Kennedy's suave television charm.

Today the media is controlling who wins the nomination and the election in several ways. One method is withholding information and using editorial prejudice to positively influence opinion about candidates. Two documented cases exemplify this. First, the Clinton/Lewinsky scandal unreported by major broadcast and print outlets until Drudge's persistence forced the issue to headlines and impeachment of the President. Second, the New York Times failure to print an article deemed damaging concerning the Obama/ACORN relationship which may have brought a different election outcome and it took the whimsical undercover video by James O'Keefe to finally destroy the organization.

The second method of influence is the prejudicial nature of coverage of candidates. For example, *The Project for Excellence in Journalism and Harvard University's Joan Shorenstein Center on the Press, Politics and Public Policy* conducted a study of 5,374 media narratives about the presidential candidates from January 1 through March 9, 2008. The study found that Obama received 69% favorable coverage and Clinton received 67%, compared to only 43% favorable media coverage of McCain. An October 29, 2008 study found 29% of stories about Obama to be negative, compared to 57% of stories about McCain being negative.

Finally, my last concern regarding media influence on politics is the pervasive use of public opinion polls. With every candidate announcement regarding potential Republican candidates a comparison poll is published. On NBC News May 26th nightly program speculation around Palin's presidential announcement was offset by a poll showing candidate positioning, with Romney in the lead. The media has given far more coverage to Romney, Gingrich, and Palin than CPAC straw poll winner Ron Paul and Tea Party favorites Cain and Bachman.

With an election 15 months away the media is focused on manipulating public opinion to control an outcome. Imagine what our election process would be like if there were no polls, no television pundits, and no scandalous coverage. Imagine speeches and debates, presented factually, without media editorial. I am not asserting to curtail freedom of the press, but instead push to present unedited coverage, eliminate polling, and present opinion as such, not news.

Soldiers v Winehouse (8/3/2011)

This past week I was riding with my daughter Haley talking about events of the week when I asked her if she knew who Amy Winehouse was. About two weeks ago Amy Winehouse died of an overdose and I had never heard of her, you probably haven't either. What intrigued me more was the amount of media coverage her death received. I watch the NBC Nightly News and they gave at least three minutes to this celebrity, focusing on a lifestyle of degradation wrought with drugs and alcohol. My daughter impressed me with her next question, "did you see the Facebook post about this?"

I asked her to explain as I had no idea what she was talking about. Haley went on to share a girl had posted about Amy Winehouse versus the soldiers who died in the same week. Essentially, this is the same issue bothering me. Receiving no media coverage were the U.S. soldiers who gave their lives in Afghanistan, Iraq, Yemen, and Libya.

Since 2002 thousands of soldiers have died fighting in our Presidents' war on terror. These are funded by, but not declared wars by Congress and in my opinion Bush and Obama along with the entire Senate and House can be blamed for these deaths. Prior to Obama's Presidency the major networks would publish the names of the soldiers who died each day and give coverage to the IEDs and bombings taking the lives of our sons and daughters. Part of Obama's election platform was the withdrawal of troops and shutting down the wars, but the opposite has happened with as many lives lost on his watch as Bush's.

I puzzle why we have U.S. soldiers dying on foreign soil and speculate the following: Iraq – to install democracy, Afghanistan – to stop Al Queda, Libya – to remove Qhadaffi, and Yemen – to protect human rights. All of these theaters are U.N. sanctioned and fought without a declaration of War by the Congress. Therefore, our soldiers are policeman, not upholding the Constitutional premise of protection against enemies foreign and domestic, especially since Osama Bin Laden was killed and the mission accomplished.

The Gulf of Tonkin taught us politicians will lie to create wars. I must now questions the policies of our government, and more personally I wonder if I would allow the government to send my sons to a questionable war. Of most concern is the media stopped questioning the reason for these wars and it now appears a meaningless, drugged up 27-year old British citizen deserves more coverage than our youth fighting a politicians' war.

Republican Chumps (09/07/11)

It is amazing how the media handles the messages from the candidates for Republican presidential nomination. Unfortunately, only "The View" and the evening news can deliver a message people will understand as most Americans will never tune into a debate. I personally believe Oprah Winfrey had more to do with the election of Senator Barak Obama than the debates and job qualifications. By comparison Hillary Clinton was far more qualified and should have taken the Democrat nomination, but she was trumped by Oprah's afternoon television show.

In Iowa last month the two winning candidates were Bachmann and Paul. However, the media spent the weekend reporting on Perry and whether he would enter the campaign. Maybe looks have more to do with the process than records, or an agenda exists behind the scenes to drive a certain candidate to the top? For instance, when Gingrich announced his campaign the media immediately began unraveling campaign contribution paperwork and essentially destroyed the campaign before it started. Likewise, questions were raised concerning Bachman's conflict between using Fannie Mae versus her opposition to the organization.

In sharp contrast, Perry has been heralded by the media as the savior to the Republican Party; the only electable candidate. Similarly Romney has maintained headlines as a contender and every effort is made to make this a two-horse race. However, under scrutiny these two candidates are far more questionable than Bachman, Paul, Cain, or the rest of the field.

Most people don't realize Perry's significant personal contributions to the Democrat party. He was formerly the Democrat Representative for Haskell County, Texas, state director of the Al Gore Presidential campaign in 1988, and in 1993 documented his enthusiastic support for Hillary Clinton's proposed health care program. By far Perry's worst action was his February 2007 executive order forcing every sixth-grade girl to submit to a three-jab regimen of the Gardasil vaccine. This decision undermines parental authority and one must wonder how such a mandate regarding a newly approved drug with unforeseen side-effects could benefit his state's citizens.

Romney is currently among the media top-ranked candidates although he skips debates and passes on appearances where voters could confront his record. Mitt Romney, as governor of Massachusetts, passed a health-care plan providing socialized medicine for its citizens. Regarding his jobs and economic performance, under Romney's leadership Massachusetts has a weak comparative economic performance of the state, one of the worst in the country.

I titled this column "Republican Chumps" for a reason; to highlight the fallacies of the contenders and question why so many are willing to blindly follow polls and "The View" to determine their Presidential nominee. I argue candidates Perry and Romney fail under scrutiny. The other candidates are only "unelectable" when ABC, NBC, and CBS make the decision on the voter's behalf. Today the "chumps" are the candidates; tomorrow the "chumps" will be the uninformed voters.

9-11 (9/21/2011)

I planned to write this column about three weeks ago, feeling it would be prophetic. However, due to personal time constraints I did not have a chance to get pen to paper until this past weekend. By then my worst fears were materializing; the media created frenzy around "potential threats." One must understand the premise of false terror and political needs to keep feeding the "monster". George Orwell explains this in *1984* as Emmanuel Goldstein; America's Goldstein is Al-Qaeda.

My heart goes out to all families who lost loved ones on September 11, 2001. Likewise, my heart goes out to the other losses in the same year and annually since then. Statistics make a case for where real threats lie, not the hype pushed at us every evening and in newspapers. On September 11th there were 3,116 Americans killed in the four airliner incidents. The Department of Homeland Security did not exist, and we were not at war in Iraq or Afghanistan.

By comparison in 2001 there were 17,448 alcohol related fatalities and 42,116 total traffic fatalities – more than ten times the number killed the morning of 9/11. In 2001 there were 16,037 murders and 90,863 rapes. The numbers show far more people were killed in 2001 by preventable causes than the significant events of that morning. However, like any tragedy the knee-jerk reaction was to mobilize the U.S. military to capture Saddam Hussein and Osama Bin Laden. History reflects Saddam had nothing to do with the attacks and it took nearly ten years to flush Bin Laden out of a luxury home in Pakistan. Meanwhile twice as many military personnel have been killed as the number of deaths that morning and an unstoppable monster called "Department of Homeland Security" now employs 200,000 and has a budget of $98 billion dollars. Sadly, even with this monumental effort to fight the "war on terrorism" preventable deaths occur and the civil rights of ordinary Americans are violated daily as collateral damage to the Patriot Act and DHS overreaching tactics to ensure safety.

I grew up in the Cold War, believing a nuclear winter would start in 20 minutes; similarly our children are growing up in a government induced façade of terrorism occurring any minute. Willfully new generations have learned to submit to security scans at public events, show papers, and give away freedoms. On the twentieth anniversary of 9/11, ten years from now, will we be living a pre-9/11 lifestyle or one of further submission? The next time you see law enforcement violating any American's 4th Amendment Rights – executing searches of vehicles, bags, and even identification – ask yourself what the real threat is: government or foreign terrorists.

11 TAXES

Death and Taxes Redux (4/13/2011)

Attending funerals I reflect on death, and although inevitable we deny our mortality one statement that intrigues me is the saying, "Only two things are known; death and taxes." I know with certainty I will die and everyone around me will die, someday. Of course cause of death cannot be predicted but risks associated with death can be minimized and each of us tries to live with a goal of prolonging life and we fight death with all of our might but cannot stop its inevitability. Taxes, however, are not an absolute, but we evolved to accept taxes part of our being, just like death. Instead of continually working toward ending this other 'absolute' in our lives our society seems willing to perpetuate this self-destructive mechanism upon ourselves.

Taking a step back, maybe a better word for tax would be "privilege payment". We pay for the privilege of living in a civilized society, and this argument could be made throughout human history. Most of us are willing to contribute a nominal amount of our individual efforts to support the purported common good of the society in which we live. I accept there is a cost to civilization as I expect infrastructure for safe water, sewage disposal, defense, and transportation.

Regardless of the specifics of the individual line items that we agree to tax ourselves for, we should constantly examine the necessity. I choose to minimize the risks I take in my daily life, exercise, eat well and therefore am hopefully prolonging my life and cheating death. I argue that we no longer do the same regarding taxes and instead readily acquiesce to taxing our individual efforts and allowing the state to control and disburse them. I assert we have voluntarily enslaved ourselves to an entity that we may not be able to escape.

Death is inevitable; the process of self-destruction through taxation is not. Taxes are acceptable when presented with a true cost and benefit analysis, a clear exit strategy from the tax, and a method to provide for checks and balances against a tax. If you were taking an inventory of your personal health in an effort to ensure you were prolonging your life you would question every risk, every activity, and eliminate those that are harming you. This same analysis must be performed frequently and regularly regarding taxes. We must question every dollar that is spent and be willing to take tough measures to eliminate waste, just as you would do personally.

12 WAR AND TERRORISM

Terrorism(1/13/2010)

Lately the news has focused on the Christmas Day underwear bomber and his attempt to destroy Northwest Flight 253 landing at Detroit. Fortunately, no lives were lost. However, I believe Umar Farouk Abdulmutallab succeeded as he has returned our focus to terrorism when considering the definition as "a state of fear and submission." Sadly though, I would offer that citizens in America are not fearful, but instead subject to fear-mongering by the media and the government.

On September 12, 2001 I believe we were all stunned and wondered, "how could this happen?" President Bush moved to create a huge new government spending program with the formation of the Department of Homeland Security and the expansion of the Transportation Security Administration. The first DHS Secretary, Tom Ridge, created the threat level designations to identify the probability of attack, but it remains the same color, "Orange", with no quantitative definition. In the post September 11th world we dutiful gave up civil rights in the name of safety, subjecting ourselves to demeaning searches at airports like removing our shoes, forcing little old ladies to forfeit knitting needles, and watching our children cry as they pass through the process. The ultimate idiocy came with the subjection of infant formula and breast milk to potential disposal.

From there, the paranoia spread to other parts of our lives, all under the guise of the "state of fear." We now attend sporting events and pass through metal detectors and have bags searched. Regardless of all the post September 11th expansion of technologies and counter-terrorism intelligence agencies, President Obama admitted there was a system failure; exemplifying the quote, "insanity is doing the same thing over and over and expecting a different outcome." But, like predecessors, President Obama and DHS Secretary Napolitano have proposed further expansion of security; spending monies on new high-tech imaging machines, explosive sniffers, more databases for comparing intelligence, and increasing TSA. Somehow they expect this will bring a different outcome, but yet they are repeating the same things.

In the new 2010 environment I have noted a radical shift in public opinion, there is no confidence in the government's plans this time. Thus, we the people have caught on to the charade, doing the same thing repeatedly will not bring a different outcome. Even media sources supporting this Administration have had a plethora of critical columnists and articles examining these new security proposals. Furthermore, citizens are finally showing outrage over the proposed invasiveness of new search techniques and enhanced screening.

Handling terrorism is difficult, but it is war. Unfortunately it is not like wars of the past where the enemy wore a different color or fought along geographical boundaries. In this politically correct world it has been made incorrect to reference a "war on terror" for fear of inflaming those who attack us. I prefer to look at the problem from an economic and statistical standpoint and question why certain terrorists are unsuccessful. I recognize there are two contrasting views regarding how security and safety is delivered. One opinion is to willingly submit to any search in the name of safety and the other is to minimize the invasiveness to the average person and instead profile certain groups. I think we also have to use quantitative values and look at cost versus benefit of different methods. Lastly, if real terrorism were to occur I do not think any amount of effort could be done to stop it.

Terrorism – Part II (1/20/2010)

Last week I shared on overview of terrorism in the last ten years and my concerns over losing civil liberties to the perception of safety; prompted by the Christmas Day underwear bomber. I offered a solution to fighting terrorism based on quantitative values and cost benefit, primarily recognizing if terrorism were to occur I do not think any amount of effort could be done to stop it.

In MBA School my professor in Economics asked us to consider how the number of exits on an airliner is determined. With 250 or more passengers, it seems there should be more than eight doors on board for evacuation. But, upon examination, it is quickly realized a door cannot be placed in every row of the aircraft because the cost to build the airplane would be exorbitant. Thus, an acceptable level of loss has been determined to offset the cost benefit of adding more doors to an airliner. A recent statistic I saw showed the probability of an American being involved in a domestic terrorism event in an 80-year life span is 1 in 80,000, whereas the probability of involvement in a car accident is 1000 times greater. Recent proposals focused on fighting terrorism through government expansion and spending billions. Statistically those monies would be more justified on automobile and highway safety to save more lives.

Recently, one of my family members said we should all just subject ourselves to a strip and body cavity search; similar to current enhanced imaging systems proposals. If we have such searches, how will failure to stop terrorism be defended. In contrast, others have proposed more specific profiling by race, gender, and religious belief. I certainly do not believe a complete subjection of us to invasive searching will eliminate all potential threats, nor do I believe specific racial or religious profiling will eliminate threats either. Another family member even proposed requiring all Americans to carry a gun, even on airliners. Outrageous as it sounds, quite frankly I believe the threat of terror, at least in America, would disappear.

I believe our security priorities are misplaced, focusing on airlines, public attractions, and sporting events. If I were a terrorist I would synchronize multiple bombings at shopping malls or Wal-Mart's across the country. I would consider blowing up parts of the national pipeline infrastructure; these pipelines traverse thousands of miles of rural countryside, cannot be guarded, and yet would stop the flow of petroleum products and cripple the economy. To blow up a plane, I would just jump the fence and plant explosives on regional jet serving the airlines. I would focus on terror, more like the pirates off the coast of Somalia. My point is there are many opportunities for terrorism, 99.9% cannot be prevented. Thus, there is a point where we have to fight back, secure ourselves, and use common sense.

During the last nine years we have adapted to the constant threat of terrorism, and it has become comedic. The terrorists have not stopped, nor will they as they are fueled by a religious hatred most of us cannot understand. Our government has chosen to spend billions of dollars, create new agencies, deploy new technologies, harass law-abiding American citizens, and blame other countries, but yet cannot stop a known terrorist from entering the country or exercising his threat. As citizens we have traded civil liberties for perceived safety and gained nothing in return. The same terrorism threat exists today as it did ten years ago, but yet we pay the personal price for the ineptness of those who claim they can protect us.

Hypocrisy (03/30/2011)

I consider hypocrisy to be the most appalling and disgusting action someone can take. I believe examples abound like politicians campaigning for family values then engaging in affairs, organized religious leaders looking away from rape by their clergy, preachers wrapped in wealth, or global warming followers driving jets and SUVs. Many on the right are struggling with the hypocrisy of the press; their basis of accusations of liberal bias against the mainstream media. Out of fairness, our media has never been held accountable for any reporting, no matter how inaccurate. With the Libyan conflict though it appears a "wink-wink" of approval has been made to the current administration.

In December 2007, Senator Obama said: "[the] president does not have power under the Constitution to unilaterally authorize a military attack in a situation that does not involve stopping an actual or imminent threat to the nation." Shortly thereafter Senator Obama was supported by Senator Joe Biden who pledged to start impeachment proceedings against President Bush if Iran were attacked without congressional approval. Ironically, we find ourselves with the hypocrisy of our President and Vice President doing exactly what they accused Bush of doing. On March 19, 2011 President Obama stated, "Today we are part of a broad coalition. We are answering the calls of a threatened people. And we are acting in the interests of the United States and the world."

Hypocritically the question must be raised as to how Obama could make such a statement, and ignore his prior assertions of Presidential authority. Over the last several weeks uprisings have occurred throughout the Middle East, starting with the self-immolation of a fruit stand worker in Tunisia. Each of the middle-eastern governments has turned on its citizens: Tripoli, Yemen, Bahrain, Libya, and of course our oil-rich ally Saudi Arabia. While the President had psychic-like success with his NCAA basketball picks his reason to start a war with a meaningless dictator remains a mystery. Whether or not I agree with Mohammar Qhaddaffi, Libya is a sovereign nation entitled to manage her affairs, or the same principles shall apply to China, Korea, Venezuela, and most of the middle-east. Protected by our media it is easy to see the quick dismissal of the hypocrisy of the situation, as a lover will always look away. "Hypocrisy is a fashionable vice, and all fashionable vices pass for virtue," – Moliere (1622-1673).

Can I wear my Shoes Now? (5/4/2011)

Sunday night I was on my way home from Atlanta tuned in to CNN when I heard the President planned an unprecedented press conference around 10:40pm. My wife and I speculated on possibilities, "what could be so important?" Jokingly I offered maybe Osama bin Laden was dead, but that certainly was not worth a late night press conference. Of course, if your poll numbers have fallen to historic lows and your re-election campaign was prematurely announced weeks ago then this could be the much needed booster shot.

I argue, "who cares?" Eight or nine years ago the death of Osama bin Laden may have had material impact. For nearly 10 years we have been given the boogeyman of threat, Bin Laden and his minions trying to harm us. Of course, Orwell would not have given up his government boogeyman, Emmanuel Goldstein, because he was the necessary fuel for the government machine. Bin Laden, like Goldstein, is a necessary enemy of the state; serving to distract, unit e and focus the people away from the true issues. Bush brought as bin Laden, a desperate politically troubled president has eliminated him. Reminding us how important it is not to piss off our enemies, the United States is treating Osama bin Laden's body in "accordance with Islamic practice," a White House official says. If this man was our enemy I assert his body be publicly hung in Times Square and treated to a ticker tape parade, unless of course, no body exists and this is a diversion.

So, the real question the next time I board an airplane is, "can I wear my shoes now?" If Bin Laden is dead I assume this means we can pull out of Afghanistan this week and bring our troops home since we spent billions of dollars chasing this idiot through caves, not unlike Bill Murray and the *Caddyshack* gopher. Sadly, the media was quick to report ramped up security efforts, more scanning, and began fear-mongering possible Al Qaeda retaliation attacks. Give me a break, Goldstein (I mean bin Laden) is dead and now the threat level is pushed to imminent. I expect more money will have to be spent to assure Al Qaeda terrorism is minimized. I expect much focus on the White House this week, defining our President as a world-wide hero who saved humanity from an evil man, with the media acting like teen-age girls at a "Teen Beat" cover shoot. Osama bin Laden is dead; can I wear my shoes now?

War! What is it Good For? (10/19/2011)

I have been traveling lately so my ability to tune to the news has been limited. However, it appears the United States is currently in the process of creating another "Gulf of Tonkin" event to justify an attack on a sovereign nation. It is hard for me to believe I would make such an accusation, but history repeats itself and desperate politicians will do anything to maintain their power. Let's take a quick look at the facts.

First, President Obama continues to slide week after week in the public opinion polls. His own party is currently turning against him and with regularity Hilary Clinton's name is floated, via trial balloons, as a possible nominee or Biden replacement. This is a President, and party, who cannot accept the downward slide and has been working toward re-election, not governance, since January 2009.

Second, the administration has lost control of several stories and will use diversions to deflect the outcome – a classic maneuver confirmed by Hollywood in the movie "Wag the Dog." Today the administration is being investigated for two significant, impeachable events: "Fast and Furious" and

"Solyandra." The diversion playbook is far easier to play from than truthful acceptance of responsibility.

Third, questions are currently rising around the alleged plot to kill the Saudi envoy to Washington. Additionally, the world does not recognize the right of the sovereign nation of Iran, a former war ally, to build its own nuclear program. Senator Diane Feinstein over the weekend affirmed her own skepticism regarding the plot by the Mexican used-car dealer to assassinate the Saudi; however she feels after her intelligence briefing there is a case. She did continue to comment this is not the time for war with Iran and America appears to be on an unavoidable collision course.

Personally, I believe Ahmadinejad to be a ruthless dictator who should not possess nuclear weapons. However, we must draw a line and avoid a possible fifth war (Iraq, Afghanistan, Yemen, and Libya) as an attack on Iran has the potential to escalate to a nuclear event. President Obama has assured the world Iran would face the "toughest possible sanctions" for its part in the assassination plot. I suggest if there were no personal gain for his administration the President would back-channel his responses and leave pleas for public opinion out of the spotlight; quiet and decisive action is more effective than loud self-serving posturing. "War! What is it good for? Absolutely nothin'!" – Norman Whitfield.

13 MY MANIFESTO

For clarity, this is not a Ted Kaczynski style manifesto accusing those in power of destruction or lashing out to call for violence. When I wrote this, during the holidays of late 2008, I had been through significant personal struggles. About 14 months prior I had lost my job, been served with a lawsuit tied to the sale of my company, and found myself battling my ex-wife over child support reduction (i.e. out of work!). The economy had also taken a turn downward and I felt like the canary in the coal mine as my job search was hopeless.

I took a job two weeks prior to writing this as a high school honors chemistry teacher. With a salary about one-fourth of what I had previously earned I could not imagine how we would survive. In the past year I had also taken and passed both the Series 7 and Series 66, allowing me to claim I was a "Registered Investment Advisor," but who wanted to trade stocks or believed in stocks? Gaining those credentials forced me to watch CNBC, research web sites, and become an "expert" on commodities, treasuries, bonds, and currencies. I was sucked into the news. Unfortunately, the news was mostly doom and gloom.

One specific item remains in my memory from the summer of 2008, comments made by real estate brokers. In New Smyrna

Beach I had also formed a "leads" group while working on my financial advisor practice. Meeting weekly we discussed how the economy was changing, mortgage approvals were disappearing, and home sales had dropped. Specifically, I remember the realtors saying "it will come back at the first of the year." How many times did Larry Kudlow speak of "Green Shoots" in the economy and blast moves by the administration? Biden and Obama touted "jobs saved or created" as unemployment has worsened. Week after week consumers were told the economy is improving and the National Association of Realtors claimed housing bottomed. Obviously, we know none of the above was the case.

In retrospect I realize what I wrote in 2008 was my attempt to articulate *The Fourth Turning* (Strauss, William and Neil Howe). Completely unaware of this book from 11 years prior I could feel change taking place and wanted to alert the world. It is an interesting read three years later, some elements sounding outlandish but others nearly prophetic.

It Will Get Worse -Be Prepared and Take Care of Yourself
12/28/2008 – by John Nelson

My predictions for 2009 and 2010 are below. I felt compelled to put this together because I have shared these thoughts with my wife and many friends. I am bothered because I see a trend in daily newspapers and news programs to report with a degree of optimism, and then with surprise, when the news is worse than they had first reported. But, I keep finding the news is not worse than I expected.

As this year has gone by I have been concerned by current events as compared to history. Our government has bailed out defense contractors and other private companies before. In the 1930's, the press and government denied what was taking place, but yet we have the benefit of history to know how bad things were. Today there is a certain level of optimism by many people and I hear comments like, "we are Americans and we always pull through." While that statement may be true, I feel concern to blind acceptance that things are always going to be ok. Throughout this article I make references to natural disasters and other external events. I feel today's economic issues are similar in that external forces are going to impact individual lives. If you ascertain nothing else from this writing I hope it is that the most significant economic changes in decades are currently occurring and preparing for the worst possible outcome will aid you in dealing with that possibility. Like all predictions or theories on trends, I may be wrong about the severity, it may be better or worse, or about the timing, events may come sooner or later. Regardless, I hope to convey concern and suggest preparation.

First, I want to provide some background information. I do not have cable television, I do not watch local news, and I do not read newspapers. On a daily and weekly basis I gather my news and opinions from the following sources:

- Daily
    - Bloomberg (http://www.bloomberg.com) – I first review world markets, particularly Asia and Europe just prior to going to bed and when I first wake. Second, the news wire provided here is far superior to any other source available
    - Drudge Report (http://www.drudgereport.com) – a great link to numerous worldwide news articles
    - Peak Oil (http://www.peakoil.com) - a link to various energy, climate change, policy, and other news articles
    - Kirk Report (http://www.kirkreport.com) – Kirk is a day trader and offers stock information. But, he also links to a huge number of financial articles and opinions focusing on Fed and other central bank policies
    - Economic Populist (http://www.economicpopulist.org) – Average people's opinions about what is currently taking place. Of most interest are the specifics of research

including graphs, data, charts and details to defend positions. Short articles, highly informative.
    - Seeking Alpha (http://www.seekingalpha.com) – Similar to Economic Populist
    - Yahoo Finance Home Page (http://finance.yahoo.com/) – What the average person sees for headlines
    - NBC Nightly News (Podcast) – download video each day and watch following morning
    - CNBC Fast Money (Podcast) – download video each day and watch the following morning
    - BBC Global News (Podcast) – download and usually listen the next day
- Weekly
    - Kunstler Cast (Podcast) – James Howard Kunstler weekly podcast. Focus is on the end of suburbia due to changes with fossil fuels
    - Bob's Gold Price Column (http://goldprice.org/bob) – what the doom and gloomers think about gold and inflation
    - Matt Simmons (http://www.simmons.com) – an energy expert

Change is taking place around us. If you had told me ten years ago that I might find myself living in a situation where I would not have power for 5-10 days, not be able to go to the grocery store to buy food – especially refrigerated items, I would find lines at gas stations, or buildings around me would be boarded up taking on a third world look, I would have laughed! However, I have lived through that situation in the summer of 2004 in New Smyrna Beach due to the hurricanes Charley, Frances, and Jean. From that experience I re-evaluated what it meant to be prepared. I thought I had everything I needed to survive: a couple of gallons of water, a bow saw, candles and a few flashlights. I learned how naïve I was. Since then, I have added a generator, chain saw and spare chains, lanterns, camping gear, stockpiles of gasoline each June, regular testing of the generator, and many other items.

Am I crazy or am I prudently prepared? Any resident of the state of Florida who does not keep minimum supplies is living in a state of denial. Other disasters and events have struck in the last 25 years in the United States and elsewhere – how prepared would you be to take care of your family?

Northridge Earthquake
Hurricane's Katrina, Charley, Andrew, Hugo, Floyd, etc
Coal Ash Levee break in Tennessee
Devastating tornadoes
Mount St. Helen's
Christmas Tsunami in Indonesia
Rogue wave – Daytona Beach 1996 (or so)
Springtime flooding in the Midwest
Terrorist attacks of 9/11/2001
Rodney King riots
Heat wave in Europe killing hundreds in France
War in Sarajevo, a beautiful Olympic city
Cholera outbreaks in Africa, 2008

My point is disasters and upheavals occur regularly, and without warning. Our ability to take care of ourselves is what matters in each case. One need only picture scenes from the news of how Hurricane Katrina victims responded versus the same, significant, devastation from Hurricane Charley in Punta Gorda, Florida and the importance of proper and prudent preparation becomes apparent. More importantly, self-sufficiency and the ability to survive without reliance on others or civil authorities is incredibly apparent.

Most citizens in the United States have lost the ability to think and be self-sufficient for themselves. Take an automobile owner's manual from the 1960's and compare it to today, 40 years later. My 1967 Mustang has details on lubricating the chassis, changing a tire, performing valve adjustments, and other maintenance. Today's owner's manual states the warranty will be voided if the work is not performed by an authorized service center. I would assert the average person, especially Generation X or Y, will call roadside assistance and wait 90 minutes to have a tire changed instead of taking 10 minutes and performing the work themselves. Furthermore, if food becomes an issue of concern I believe most citizens will be at a loss. They will not know how to grow or kill food due to the basic belief that food comes from the grocery store. I had a friend share his concerns about the differences today versus the Great Depression – in the 30's he feels a person would have given his place in a food line to another out of kindness and sacrifice. Today, he feels your life is at risk due to the selfishness of most people and their inability to survive without assistance.

One problem society seems to face is forgetting our history. As recently as summer 2008 gasoline prices were over $4.00/gallon. Behaviors were changing: scooter and motorcycle riding was up, SUV purchases declined catastrophically, people moved closer to work or considered changing jobs to reduce commutes, trips were combined, leisure travel was eliminated, and overall there was a general trend toward conservation. In 1974, due to political events, Americans had to ration gasoline resulting in huge shortages. Odd and even days were used to determine purchases and none could be made on Sunday's. An immediate move toward smaller cars was made. To a lesser extent, the same problems arose in the early 1980's and panic over dependence on oil again ensued.

During 2008, many newsworthy events have taken place, but without the benefit of seeing them all at once it is hard to imagine the economic and societal decay taking place around us:

- Rice and flour shortages on the west coast as Asian populations understood shortages oversees
- Rising global food prices due to US policies on ethanol
- Gas shortages in the Southeast US due to supply problems after hurricanes
- Over a dozen airlines went into bankruptcy or out of business
- Major brand stores went bankrupt (Steak n Ale, Circuit City, Linens and Things, etc)

- More than 170 banks failed as of 12/1/2008
- Christmas holiday spending was the lowest in 40 years
- Year over year housing price decline of 13%
- Unemployment claims are at their highest in 25 years
- Diminishing new job opportunities, compounding unemployment problems
- Dow Jones high of 14,000 in October 2007, low of 7570 in November 2008 – 45% erasure of value
- 1 out of 10 mortgages is in default or behind on payments
Rising defaults on credit cards and car loans

Throughout the year, news sources have reported events with an element of denial or ultimately surprise when the data become available. Just this week, on 12/26/08 I heard the following reported on Fox News Network:

"Retailers were surprised at the worse drop in holiday sales in over 40 years."

They went on to report possible reasons such as: there were six less shopping days between Thanksgiving and Christmas, a holiday snowstorm that kept consumers away from malls. The comical reporting came next: some consumers may be concerned about job loss and not spending as much, credit cards are maxed out and no new credit is available. Last but not least, they reported that the economy of the United States is consumer based and that the total GDP – the production of all products and services – is 70% consumerism. Thus, without the citizens consuming the economy is grinding to a halt. 'They' need to force 'us' to start consuming.

Our problem as a country and with our current economic situation is we do not make anything that anyone else wants. We make money and recycle it within our own borders. Thus, growth is a fantasy based on a false reality. The best example is real estate over the last six years; the rapid growth had nothing to do with a true increase in value due to supply and demand. Instead, the easy availability of credit perpetuated a debt-based drive toward home ownership where prior lending standard required 20% down (leveraging of 5:1) now allowed 5% down (leveraging 20:1). Finally, these standards were reduced to 0% or even -5% down – the equivalent of infinite leveraging. This was a house of cards doomed to collapse. During this time, the media constantly reported that housing prices would recover within a three to six months. This took place throughout late 2007 and all through 2008.

I had to set the background for where we have been before I felt I could make predictions on where we are going. My synopsis is below with a predictive narrative and finally recommendations to plan for the next 2-3 years:

- Housing – there will be no recovery in housing before the end of 2011. Housing prices in some areas inflated as much as 2%/month (24% per annum). Historically, housing rise at a rate equal to or just above inflation. Thus, it will take 10-15 years to work back to the 2006 highs. This is compounded further by an inventory of 4 million homes for sale when historic inventories are between 2 and 2.5 million. Last but not least, lending is not available to purchase homes with debt.
- Credit – Consumers will not have credit readily available until late 2009 or early 2010. Our consumption based economy will remain frozen until the spending engine can restart.
- Equity Markets – The Dow and S&P500 remain overvalued. Current estimates of average earnings for the S&P are about $55. Thus, the S&P is trading on a forward multiplier of about 18-20. Analysts have consistently overvalued earnings and multipliers throughout 2008. Many blue-chip, dividend paying stocks are trading closer to a multiplier of 7-10. Historic norms are 14-15. Thus, using a multiplier of 10, the S&P should be at 550.
- Currency – The Fed has printed huge sums of monies. Taxpayers generally pay about $1 trillion per year in federal income taxes. In the last 12 months Congress and the Fed have promised about $7 trillion in bail outs, stimulus, and balance sheet increases. As large as the numbers are, a huge

deflationary move has taken place due to the erasure of debt, thus offsetting some of the severity of the inflationary monetary policies. If other governments reduce lending rates and increase currencies, the dollar will not be devalued. However, inflation is inevitable.

- Oil and Energy – Oil has plunged to the mid-$30s from a high of $147/bbl in July 2008. Commodity markets tend to overshoot both directions to the high side and the low side while supply and demand realign. The issue with oil is not one that we are going to have no oil. Instead, the marginal cost to produce each subsequent barrel of oil is higher than the preceding barrel. This is the root concept of Peak Oil; supply will not keep pace with demand. Hubbert's peak in the early 1970's in the United States is well-documented and the same will apply to world supply and demand. During the peak there will be wild oscillations in prices, supply, and demand. We are at the beginning of the peak and experiencing the swings.
- Climatic Change – the Green lobby is promoting huge expenditures due to perceived global warming. Regardless of political views, climatic change appears to be taking place. The summer Arctic ice in 2008 melted at a rate that allowed transit across the polar ice cap from North America to Asia and Europe that had not been possible due to being previously frozen for the last thousand years. Plants not exposed for a thousand years appeared this summer. The Greenland Ice shelf is melting at an unprecedented rate and the risk of a significant piece sliding into the ocean is increasing daily. There is less snow and ice to reflect sunlight causing a possible natural exponential warming trend that cannot be reduced. Salinity values in the North Atlantic are changing, thus impacting the flow of the gulf stream and the natural cooling process in the northern hemisphere. These changes may be normal on a geological time scale which we cannot measure or they may be due to increases in carbon in the atmosphere driven by man made changes in the last 150 years. Regardless, they appear to be taking place at a

significant rate. This climatic change will impact coast cities, farming communities, water supplies, and world hunger throughout the rest of the century.

- Geopolitical Issues – The middle-east remains an area of concern with religious based hatred of western civilizations being a catalyst for terrorism and oil policy changes. Israel has ramped up hostilities in Gaza Strip and India and Pakistan are both nuclear powers with increasing hostilities. Russia is establishing herself again as a world power, particularly with an interest on controlling energy and pipelines feeding Europe.
- Politics in the United States – A new, inexperienced president will try to create policies to save the country as he promised during the campaigns. At the same time, the House Speaker, Nancy Pelosi, has a strong liberal agenda that she believes she can now accomplish including: union supported legislation, national health care, increased taxes and wealthy producers, and a general move to a more socialized country. President Obama will work to pass legislation to make owning firearms more difficult, most likely through taxation on ammunition or illegality of personally possessing ammunition like Switzerland successfully implemented in 2007. He will try to create 3 million jobs, but that will not impact the economy for 5-7 years. He will support another stimulus package and saving the auto makers, moves that will further add to our debts.

In 2009, I see a temporary stock market rally based on the euphoria of a new president and false confidence that he can implement programs that will save the country and the average person without significant ownership or pain on their part. The House will pass another stimulus package which will not stimulate the economy as consumers hoard cash out of fear of losing their jobs. The president will be tested by events in the middle-east that will ultimately result in him appearing weak as nothing can be done to prevent the hostilities that have brewed for thousands of years. Throughout first quarter 2009 unemployment will continue to rise at unprecedented rates, reaching 10% by April and 12% by July. Housing prices will continue to decline as lending is not available. As unemployment increases, consumers will further reduce spending worried about their own future and possible job losses. Those that have a job will be reluctant to consider moving and will not purchase existing or new homes.

Company earnings will decline as consumer spending slows and worldwide spending continues to decline. The stock market will test new lows at 7000, 6000, and finally 5000 before settling into a period of flat trading between 5000 and 6500 for three to five years. The media will begin to report, with surprise, a rise in consumer prices and producer prices in late 2009 as inflation begins to take hold due to the failed policies of the Fed and Congress. Housing again will not restart because lending rates will increase from 5% back to rates not seen since the early 1980's of 12-14%. Oil prices will also increase for three reasons: a devaluation of the dollar against world currencies, reduction in supply from OPEC to gain a foothold back to the $80/bbl level they desire, and the previously discussed middle-east tensions causing further supply concerns. Hyperinflation will take hold in early 2010 causing President Obama to sign executive orders for price controls on basic staples such as milk, bread, flour, and sugar. Ensuing hoarding and shortages will occur as citizens try to stockpile supplies in anticipation of shortages. Riots and general unrest, particularly in New Orleans, Detroit, Washington DC, and Los Angeles will be reported. These riots will occur because the average population has not been taught how to survive or be self-sufficient. Instead, they have been raised as consumers with all of the requirements of civility readily available at a nearby Wal-Mart.

My recommendations are to prudently prepare. Just like an impending storm in a coastal Florida city, preparation will be the key to survival. Some of these changes will happen slowly, others rapidly. Preparation may be as simple as just thinking about what might happen. Regardless, good preparation may involve purchasing or stockpiling goods not normally kept.

- Investments should be made over the short term with sales into rallies and purchases in the troughs
- Short the S&P with the SDS if the symbol goes below 80 (or 85) and sell when above 110. You can repeat this strategy many times
- Reduce debt – do not take on new debt
- Refinance at historically low interest rates. They will be at 10-15% in the future. Refinance below 5.25%. You will not see this again in your lifetime.
- Do not make debt based purchases when rates are rising or above 9%. The monthly cost of cash flow is 30% minimum
- Hoard cash – it will diminish in value, but cash is king. Cash provides options.
- Make wise purchases – do not buy luxury or un-needed items
- Adequate preparation for 7-10 days of survival without power should be a minimum requirement regardless of where you live
- Tools for debris removal, house repair, and fixing and repairing household appliances should be available
- Basic first aid kits should be kept in all cars and at home
- Personal relationships should be made with local doctors and police to facilitate first priority care for you and your family
- Consideration should be given to a safe haven, a place to go
- A family plan should exist in the event of communication failures (no cell phones)
- Arming with a shotgun, rifle, and pistol should be done. Weapons can be used for protection, hunting, or trade if needed. They will last a lifetime and if political policy changes they may become very valuable
- Further preparation should be made in the face of inflation – spend an extra $20/week grocery shopping on staples and dry goods
- Ammunition, Gold, and Jack Daniels will be the currency of the future. Whether or not you own a gun, purchase one to

two boxes of shotgun shells, 9 mm, or .38 cal ammunition monthly. Purchase a bottle of Jack Daniels monthly. All can be sold later.

- Learn basic first aid
- Consider solar power supply options and re-evaluate power tools owned to be rechargeable
- Explore basics of wind and solar electricity to charge power tools and items to maintain basic civility
- Inverters that convert 12-volt battery supplies to 110 to use with modern amenities
- Find outdoor solar lights at garage sales or store sale's racks and use as indoor lighting by moving the solar panel outdoors and the lights inside
- Accumulate good camping gear – lanterns, sleeping bags, stove, and tent. Camp for a weekend or longer periods to understand what it is like to live without basics. Add to gear over time to improve survivability. Every time I camp it seems I want more flashlights, batteries, knives, propane, and lanterns to make my life easier. If it rains I want to stay dry – bags, containers, tarps, etc.
- Blankets, jackets, scarves, gloves
- Store all tools, gear, in organized easy to take with you containers
- Ensure tetanus and other immunizations are up to date
- Stockpile basic medicines such as Aspirin and Benadryl, iodine tablets for radiation exposure
- Keep Mylar, Duct Tape, chain saw blades, tarps, nails, screws, tie wraps for emergency repairs and protection against weather, gas hazards

All of the above can be part of your basic lifestyle and should help you feel prepared without feeling like a nutso preparing for the end of the world. Choose to consider living with the idea that Wal-Mart and the grocery store may not be there tomorrow.

Test your preparation with the following questions:

- I live in a winter storm area; can I survive the cold and snow without power for 7 days?
- A tree lands on my house during a rainstorm, can I make repairs on my own?
- A train derails spilling chlorine gas, what would I do?
- I am traveling and a terrorist attack occurs, communication is cut with my family. What would we do?
- Price controls take place and bread costs $10/loaf. Can I cook and survive?
- Social unrest is occurring and the National Guard has implemented curfews. Power is out and the grocery stores are closed. What would I do?
- Gasoline is available in rations of 20 gallons per month, what would I do?
- We are evacuating to another locale due to …….I find myself in tense situations while buying gasoline, what would I do?
- A nearby levee breaks flooding our town and my neighborhood, what would I do?
- An earthquake occurs, or the ground shifts resulting in the collapse of my home, what would I do?

Books and websites I recommend

- "The Long Emergency", James Howard Kunstler – a rather prophetic view of what is currently happening written in 2004
- "World Made by Hand", James Howard Kunstler – a fictional look at 'life after'. After collapse of the government due to some event such as war or social disorder we are living like it is 1890 again
- "The Creature from Jekyll Island" – How the Federal Reserve was created and the control of banking over all decisions
- "Jericho" – The CBS Television series, two seasons. The writing/acting is horrible in the first few episodes but improves. It is too much like other CBS shows. However, it

strengthens. You should take away from this the relationships that form, how people deal with crisis, and the warring tribal nature that develops between towns

- "Atlas Shrugged", Ayn Rand – a fictional look at the world in a sense where producers choose to no longer be victimized by policies that take from those who make
- "Lucifer's Hammer", Larry Niven – a fictional book I read in 1979 about a meteor colliding with the earth. The hero is an engineer who prepares and survives through self-sufficiency
- Peak Oil, Life after the Crash (http://www.lifeaftertheoilcrash.net/) – Worth reviewing to gain education about possible changes in the future
- Build a Wind Turbine (http://www.mdpub.com/Wind_Turbine/index.html) – Want to build a practical windmill or solar panel – great site to see someone doing it

14 COLUMN TITLES

ABOUT THE AUTHOR

John Nelson lives in the North Georgia mountains with his wife and younger two sons, and is a father of five. Nelson is a Chemical Engineer and has an MBA. Nelson has worked as a registered engineer, high school chemistry teacher, and entrepreneur. He loves flying, reading, and spending time with his family.

www.ingramcontent.com/pod-product-compliance
Lightning Source LLC
Chambersburg PA
CBHW060250290526
45789CB00001B/272
* 9 7 8 1 4 6 3 5 3 5 5 6 8 *